LONDON: 1870–1914

A City at its Zenith

LONDON
1870-1914
A City at its Zenith

Andrew Saint

LUND
HUMPHRIES

To haunt the great city and by this habit to penetrate it, imaginatively, in as many places as possible – that was to be informed, that was to pull wires, that was to open doors, that positively was to groan at times under the weight of one's accumulations.

Henry James, preface to *The Princess Casamassima* (1886)

Contents

Preface

This book aims to present London during a momentous period of its history in a fresh way, balancing the social, the topographical and the visible aspects of the great city. London between 1870 and 1914 has earned the homage of many fine studies – some of the best of them very academic and rather negative in tone. I have felt the lack of an up-to-date, readable and well-illustrated book that embraces the whole in a positive spirit.

My interpretation of London's history in the period covered is unashamedly one of progress in the face of great odds. In almost every aspect it was a much better city in 1914 than in 1870. At a time when local autonomy in Britain has been ruthlessly downgraded and London's face is every year coarsened further by money-led developments, this story of gradual and earnest improvement may have lessons to teach.

My method has been to adopt a discursive style of narrative. This approach, plus the structure of four chronological chapters, derives from four lectures I gave for the Victorian Society in an annual series organised by Michael Hall some time back on each of the Victorian and Edwardian decades. I have enlarged and enriched the original texts of those talks and tried to purge them of excessive rhetoric. Each of the four chapters is meant to be read through from start to finish; there are no stark subdivisions within them. Subjects appear where I felt they were best suited to do so, without undue rigidity about the time-frame; some reappear, others don't. Thus political agitation and the grievous problems of poverty take up most of the second chapter but reappear briefly in the fourth; education comes at some length in the first and second chapters, briefly in the fourth; art in the first and third; suburbanisation in the first, second and fourth; transport in the fourth – and so on. The range is wide but very far from comprehensive. Omissions will easily be spotted.

Most of what I have learnt about London has been acquired over more than thirty years, on and off, working for the Survey of London. I shall always be

grateful for the privilege and luck I have enjoyed in being allowed to help carry
that august series forward; no city in the world can boast its equivalent. I thank
all my colleagues on the Survey, living and dead, for their support, collaboration
and indulgence over the years. Presumptuously perhaps, I like to think of this
book as a successor of a quite different kind to the late Francis Sheppard's *London
1808–1870: The Infernal Wen*, published as long ago as 1971. Much of that splendid
book was likewise based on the knowledge Sheppard had accumulated over his
long years as Editor of the Survey.

 I should like in the first place to thank my editors and their colleagues at Lund
Humphries, Anna Norman, Rochelle Roberts and Val Rose; Lucie Worboys who
made the layouts; my excellent copy editor, John Jervis; and the designer of the
cover, James Nunn. Susannah Stone carried out picture research for me with
speed, precision and enthusiasm. First among friends who have supported and
advised me throughout, not least over the book's appearance, is Ida Jager. Geoff
Brandwood generously took several photographs for me and allowed me to use
others by him, always without charge. Others who have helped me in one way
or another, especially over pictures, are Susie Barson, Timothy Brittain-Catlin,
Eileen Chanin, Peter Cormack, Gillian Darley, Alecsandra Raluca Dragoi, Ian
Dungavell, Hilary Grainger, John Greenacombe, Peter Guillery, Michael Hall,
Libby Horner, Nicholas Jacobs, Frank Kelsall, Sarah Milne, Jon Newman, Chris
Redgrave, Aileen Reid, Len Reilly, John Scott, Amy Spencer, Colin Thom, and last
but not least, Robert Thorne.

 Finally, warm thanks are due to two bodies in particular: the London
Metropolitan Archives, which allowed me to use their images at a greatly reduced
rate; and the Marc Fitch Fund, which made a generous grant covering the main
costs of the pictures I was obliged to purchase. The cost of illustrating books
well can be prohibitive for freelance authors these days without subsidies such
as these.

1.1 Kensington House, Baron Albert Grant's monster mansion. Built to James Knowles junior's designs in 1873–6, pulled down in 1882. (Kensington Libraries)

1

London in the 1870s

Let's begin with a house (fig.1.1). A great country house perhaps, with ample ornamental grounds and a lake? It's in the French Second Empire style, so perhaps of the 1860s? Yet, with its full third storey, isn't it rather high for a country house? And what are those tall buildings looming shadily to the right?

Those background buildings are indeed of the '60s; they are the rear of houses in Prince of Wales Terrace, Kensington. But the mansion itself belongs to the 1870s. It is one of those rare curiosities, the house that is built with high ambition and grand style yet never inhabited. Kensington House was built for Baron Albert Grant to the designs of James Knowles junior in 1873–6. It was absolutely and completely finished, with a gigantic basement, dozens of bedrooms, painted ceilings, and an orangery and skating rink in the garden. All for nothing. It was pulled down in 1882.

Albert Grant was a confidence trickster. Born Abraham Gottheimer in Dublin to a Polish-Jewish father and British mother, he became a self-made international financier, shifting between London and Paris. His first fortune was acquired through a British company called the Credit Foncier, copying a solid French concern of the same name. He was elected MP for Kidderminster in 1865 but came unstuck in the great banking crisis of 1866 and had to move abroad, where he helped finance the Galleria Vittorio Emanuele II in Milan – hence his Italian barony, which he may have bought. By 1870 Grant was back in London, floating companies of all sorts. Many were fraudulent ones whose assets were hard to value because they were far away, such as silver mines in Nevada and Utah and an unbuildable tramway route between Lisbon and Sintra. By astute financial juggling he had amassed enormous paper wealth by the time he embarked on the boastful project of Kensington House, partly built on slum property. Grant's method of ejecting tenants was to ignore the law and simply throw cash at them.

The great house started to rise, in the French taste beloved of Victorian nouveaux riches. Then came another credit crisis, less severe than 1866 but enough to catch out a gambler like Grant. Still, in 1874 he managed to get himself re-elected for Kidderminster. He also indulged in the populist gesture of buying up the gardens of Leicester Square and renewing them to Knowles's design with the cut-price cultural statuary still there today. His benefaction is recorded on the pedestal of the Shakespeare statue in the middle (fig.1.2).

But the Baron was again on the skids, and the foreclosures and lawsuits began. Somehow Kensington House got finished, and Knowles was even paid. In 1877 Grant was declared bankrupt. His paintings – including Landseers, Friths, Millais and Stanfields – were sold, but the house failed to find a bidder. It was too big, too vulgar perhaps, perhaps also out of date, so down it came. Grant went on to found one final bank, was again declared bankrupt and died in poverty in 1899. He has lived on as Melmotte in *The Way We Live Now*, the most politically pungent of all Trollope's novels. Appositely, the book appeared in 1874–5, while Kensington House was still building. Melmotte (fig.1.3) had poisoned himself long before Grant was sold up. But no one has ever doubted that this imaginary financier and fraudster, who keeps bubbles in the air through sheer effrontery and force of personality, is Grant; the publication of Trollope's wildly successful book may even have been a factor in his exposure and downfall.

1.2   Shakespeare statue, Leicester Square gardens, by Giovanni Fontana after Peter Scheemakers. Given by Baron Albert Grant, 1874.

After the collapse of 1873, so soon after that of 1866, there was a feeling that something had gone wrong in the City of London, technically and morally. Walter Bagehot's *Lombard Street*, published that same year, was a political response, calling for the Bank of England to be recognised as the lender of last resort. *The Way We Live Now* was its moral equivalent, the criticism articulated in its very title. As often in Trollope, the book presents a contrast between the author's innate conservatism and the modernisation of Victorian life, which is presented as inevitable and compelling yet tasteless and nasty. There is less of the conservative and more of the modern in *The Way We Live Now* than in most earlier Trollope novels, supplying a hard-nosed tone to the whole performance. That perhaps is a characteristic of the 1870s.

Dickens dies in 1870. Over the next decade Trollope continues to head the English fictional field alongside George Eliot, George Meredith and the upcoming

1.3 'Melmotte speculates': illustration by Lionel Grimston Fawkes for Anthony Trollope's *The Way We Live Now*, 1874–5.

Thomas Hardy – all mainly provincial in their subject matter. You can sniff the change and the new cynicism in Trollope's writing. In *The Way We Live Now*, Lady Carbury, an impoverished widow who writes trashy books to keep her head above water, receives a marriage offer from Mr Broune, editor of the *Morning Breakfast Table*. 'Now she found that he not only had a human heart in his bosom, but a heart that she could touch. How wonderfully sweet! How infinitely small!' Marie Melmotte, the financier's crabby daughter, remarks to a suitor whose family owns a castle: 'I hate old places. I should like a new house, and a new dress, and a new horse every week, – and a new lover.' Dickens never writes like that. He can denounce, he can satirise vehemently, but he never sounds jaundiced. Trollope watches from the sidelines and jabs in sarcasms.

Subversive of class, family loyalties and traditions, *The Way We Live Now* mostly takes place in London. There is the collapse of caste, as money invades everything, including the aristocratic quarters of the West End. There is the Jewish question and the woman question, new interests that Trollope shared with George Eliot. Melmotte himself is Jewish, as was Grant, and some play is made with this. The two questions even converge, when the gutsy Georgiana Longstaffe dares to break with her stuffy landed but indebted family and accept a respectable older merchant and Jew. With a dash of modernity, Trollope makes this end badly, when Georgiana is forced to break it off and marry the local curate, with whom she is miserable.

* * *

What was life like for a Londoner at this time? Avoiding the string of statistics that might anchor an objective answer to the question, here are some impressions and images.

As it happens, for London in the 1870s we have two remarkable picture books: Gustave Doré's *London: A Pilgrimage*, issued in 1872 (figs 1.4, 1.5), and the less familiar photographs published in 1877 by John Thomson as *Street Life in London* (figs 1.6, 1.7). There are similarities and differences between the books. Both are social studies of a kind, if superficial compared with the earlier publications of Henry Mayhew. Both have solid texts to go with the images; Doré's by Blanchard Jerrold (with whom he quarrelled), Thomson's largely by a young journalist and socialist called Adolphe Smith. Both concern themselves with the poor, Thomson exclusively so, while Doré includes several scenes of smart life. In their own ways both are rhetorical and contrived.

The obvious difference between them is the medium, which imposes advantages and drawbacks on each. In his wood engravings, Doré is able to depict

crowds and the swirling tide of humanity, as no photographer of the 1870s can. So we should not read the relative stillness of Thomson's photos as some token of a quietening-down from the disturbed metropolitan life portrayed by Doré. Allowing for all the posing, there is a truthfulness and realism in Thomson's photos that Doré can't match. The clothes in his pictures, for instance, cannot lie. Doré creates a dark internal world. But is it London? The buildings apart, it hardly looks so at all. Often it looks more like Paris and, as has been noticed, it looks even more like hell. Thomson's low-life characters enjoy themselves. There is hope in his photos but little hope in Doré, even when people are supposedly having fun.

Arguably you can catch in the London of the 1870s an inkling of increasing hope, of emancipation even from the constraints of the previous generation. It's only incipient: we are still far from the fin de siècle. Yet almost indiscernibly, personal lives in London seem to be becoming less grim and inhibited, freer, bolder – and more opportunistic: that is one of the messages of *The Way We Live Now*. The change is more palpable in middle-class lives, of course, than in those of the poor portrayed by Doré and Thomson.

Take Arthur Munby. On the surface Munby was a respectable law clerk working for the Ecclesiastical Commissioners. But he lived an unusual life which we only know about from his diary, published long after his death with the subtitle 'Man of Two Worlds'. Munby's *faiblesse* was picking up working women, not for sex but for emotional comfort and unjudging companionship. Often he

1.4, 1.5   Scenes from Blanchard Jerrold and Gustave Doré, *London: A Pilgrimage*, 1872. Left: 'Applying for admission at a refuge'. Right: 'Steamboats at Westminster Pier'.

1.6, 1.7 Scenes from John Thomson and Adolphe Smith, *Street Life in London*, 1877.
Above: 'Workers on the Silent Highway'.
Below: 'November Effigies', showing 'a nondescript guy, somewhat clumsily built up by a costermonger who lives in the southeast of London'. A man in women's clothes beats the drum. (LSE Digital Library)

photographed or drew them. His main flame was Hannah Cullwick, a servant whom he encountered in the street back in 1854 (fig.1.8). He kept her hidden and at arm's length for years.

Then things change. Munby describes 1870 as a 'hateful and villainous year, bloody with wars still raging, treacherous with newly broken treaties; in which the hopes of human progress . . . have at length finally died out' (presumably he is thinking of the Franco-Prussian War). Yet in 1872 he finally installs Hannah in his chambers, and next year he secretly marries her. On the surface little alters; as before, few of Munby's friends know about Hannah. In their private relationship at home they both prefer it if she dresses and behaves as a servant and he as her master, but when they go out of town they behave more like a married couple. So there is some slight easing up.

1.8   Arthur Munby and Hannah Cullwick, 16 September 1876, from a sketch by Munby. (Derek Hudson, *Munby, Man of Two Worlds*, 1972)

* * *

Munby lived on the fringes of the art world, and it's naturally in art and design and the affluent segment of society connected to that world that we can glimpse bourgeois freedom and individualism begin to emerge and express themselves.

A significant moment in the annals of art in London came in 1869, for in that year the Royal Academy transferred to Burlington House from its previous cramped premises in the National Gallery. New buildings round the forecourt followed, designed for the so-called 'learned societies' by Charles Barry junior, older son of the Houses of Parliament's famous architect, while Burlington House itself was remodelled and heightened. The National Gallery now had the opportunity to expand. A competition for its rebuilding had been won by Charles's younger and abler brother Edward. In the event only a fraction of his scheme was built. Opened in 1876, it is surely the finest portion of the Gallery (fig.1.9).

The transfer to Burlington House should have heralded a new era for the Royal Academy, yet the 1870s marked the beginnings of a decline in its status. The failure of the Academicians to elect some front-rank painters like Dante Gabriel Rossetti and Albert Moore may have had something to do with it. But there had always been good artists outside or against the Academy. Another factor was that, with more leisure, better education and a wider spread of wealth, alternative places for the public display of art could thrive.

The landmark secession was the founding of the Grosvenor Gallery in New Bond Street, patronised by leading members of the art set from Burne-Jones to Whistler. The Grosvenor's opening in 1877 is often taken as a kicking-off point for the Aesthetic Movement. Loose and vague though the movement was, that

1.9   Looking into the rooms designed by E.M. Barry at the National Gallery in 2014. (Wikimedia Commons, Diego Delsa)

did not lessen its impact. It had its roots in Pre-Raphaelitism; the phrase 'art for art's sake', cribbed from French criticism, seems first to have occurred in an essay on Blake by Swinburne of 1868. Avant-garde artists and ideas, with their intimations of individualism, passion and rebellion, had become familiar by the time the Grosvenor opened. It was over a painting shown at the Grosvenor that Ruskin was sued by Whistler in 1878 for calling him a coxcomb who asked two

1.10   Grosvenor Gallery, interior. (*Illustrated London News*, 5 May 1877)

1.11 'Art in Excelsis':
a George du Maurier
cartoon from *Punch*. 'The
Montgomery Spiffinses
have just had their
drawing room ceiling
elaborately decorated by
artistic hands. They are
much gratified by the
sensation produced upon
their friends.'

hundred guineas 'for flinging a pot of paint in the public's face'. That could hardly
have happened or attracted the attention it did if there hadn't been an established
public sense of two camps in art, the old and the new.

The Grosvenor Gallery (fig.1.10) hardly looked rebellious. The building
itself was banal, and at its outset was perhaps neither better lit nor hung than
Burlington House. But it was comfortably small and, unlike the Academy, it had
facilities – a library, a club and a basement restaurant: all places for respectable,
mixed-sex enjoyment.

The new woman, emancipated, taste-setting and increasingly found about on
her own, is a powerful theme of the 1870s. London now starts to make space for
her. Venues like the Grosvenor Gallery proliferate, as do hotels, restaurants and
large shops, and shape their facilities and looks to women's preferences. It goes
without saying that women had always played a big role in patronage and taste.
Yet there's a sense from this time of growing confidence and authority about
their involvement and influence in matters of art. Many of George du Maurier's
Punch cartoons of the 1870s address the Aesthetic Movement and the role women
played in it. If they are often caricatured as vain and scatty, that's better than the
men, who look useless and stupid (fig.1.11).

The outstanding representatives of the new woman in 1870s London are
the Garrett sisters and cousins. Their background, as often with Victorian
reformers, was liberal-evangelical, bordering over time on agnostic. The greatest
of the Garretts was Elizabeth Garrett Anderson (fig.1.12), who pioneered medical

1.12 Elizabeth Garrett
Anderson. (National
Portrait Gallery)

1.13 The New Hospital
for Women, Euston
Road, c.1914. J.M.
Brydon, architect, 1889.
Now much altered.
(Wikimedia, from
Wellcome Collection.
L0019498)

education for women and hospitals for women. After training as a doctor in the face of great prejudice, her breakthrough came with the founding of the New Hospital for Women in 1872 and the London School of Medicine for Women in 1874. In 1877 the Royal Free Hospital allowed women medical students to work on its wards, without which they couldn't get the clinical experience to qualify as doctors. After that the women's hospital went from strength to strength, eventually occupying the building that is still there on Euston Road (fig.1.13).

Hardly less impressive was Elizabeth's sister Millicent, who married the blind MP Henry Fawcett and spoke at the first public women's suffrage meeting in London in 1870 at the age of 22. Millicent's real political activity as a suffragist started later, in her widowhood. The Garrett sisters are a reminder that the new woman of the 1870s thought about more than literature, art and interiors. But such things certainly did interest them. Another sister, Agnes, along with her cousin Rhoda, founded an interior decorators' firm, which had modest success. In 1876 they produced a little manual about interiors in a series popularising the Queen Anne taste. The Garretts' book is wholly London-centred and seems aimed at the art-conscious metropolitan classes (fig.1.14).

Middle-class women were also now more willing and able to manifest their enjoyment and pleasure in public. For instance, the skating craze that suddenly smote London in 1875 seems to have had special appeal for women. Both roller

skating and ice skating were involved and relied on recent technical improvements. A newish sport, roller skating required a smooth surface, usually of cement, asphalt or timber (there was even a Marble Rink in Clapham Road), plus modern skates featuring india-rubber wheels with ball bearings. Public rinks for roller skating erupted all over fashionable London: at the Royal Aquarium and the Alexandra Palace (both newly opened in the 1870s), the Royal Agricultural Hall, the Holborn Amphitheatre, the Oxford Circus Rink (this one survives as a Salvation Army hall), the Belgrave Rink in Ebury Street, the Lillie Bridge Rink and so on. Naturally, Baron Grant had a skating rink at Kensington House. There was even a song about this 'Rinkomania' entitled *The Rink Galop*; on the cover of the sheet music, well-dressed women gallivant around the floor with just a single man in half-view (fig.1.15). The picture reminds us that for most recreations short of swimming, women did not yet change their costume.

Ice skating, an older pursuit, was technically trickier to provide outside a few unpredictable winter weeks. Attempts to establish all-year skating rinks back in the 1840s had petered out, mainly because the ice was procured by means of brine, which tended to corrode the pipes. Cashing in on the new skating craze, the inventor John Gamgee cracked the problem at his Glaciarium on the King's Road, Chelsea, using glycerine and water as his conducting agent connected to a refrigerating plant. His first rink opened to subscribers in January 1876. In a larger version that followed, Gamgee switched to sulphuric acid and ether as his conduit to keep the surface frozen. There were others in Manchester and Southport. But skaters found them chilly, and their surfaces tended to exhale a kind of icy mist.

As suddenly as the skating craze emerged, it collapsed. There were several bankruptcies and one prosecution on moral grounds – at the Empress Rink off the Edgware Road, where female ballet dancers dressed up as men. As in all crazes

of the kind, people seem simply to have got bored. By the early 1880s all Gamgee's
establishments had closed, and only a few roller rinks survived.

* * *

It is time for a look at how London was run in the 1870s. Nationally, this is a
period of comparative stability. Always there in the background are Gladstone
and Disraeli. Gladstone is Prime Minister from 1868 to 1874, when his defeat
follows the economic downturn; Disraeli then takes over until 1880. That is
different from the shifting governments of the 1850s and '60s and lends security
to the decade. Broadly speaking, this was a confident period. The recent opening
of the Suez Canal, in which Britain became the majority shareholder after some
sleight of hand in 1875, and the enfeeblement of France following its defeat by
Germany in the Franco-Prussian War, left the country stronger than ever. The

21

1.17 The Alexandra Palace in 1873, shortly before it was completed. It burnt down a fortnight after it opened and was rebuilt to a different design. (Gavin Stamp, *The Changing Metropolis*, 1984)

long agricultural depression that gripped the English countryside for the last decades of the century started around 1873 but had yet to tighten its grip.

If London's overall government meant anything in the 1870s, it meant the Metropolitan Board of Works (MBW), then at the halfway point of its existence – it ran from 1855 until 1889. The Board had never been conceived as an overall or representative government for London as a whole. It had been set up with the brief of sorting out the pressing problem of sewage disposal, which neither the existing parish vestries nor the previous commissions of sewers had managed to cope with. Proving effective at that one task, it was given others. So the Board slipped into becoming a kind of municipal government by accident.

By 1870 Joseph Bazalgette's great scheme of outfall sewers had been accomplished, but there was still much tidying up to do. Finishing off and continuing things was typical of what passed for planning just then. The previous decade had seen enormous changes to London's infrastructure. The railways had made slashing incursions into the centre, including the start of the Underground; major new streets had been driven through the densest built-up areas; the construction of the sewer system caused equal disruption.

Likewise, many public building projects started previously had yet to be finished off. The Prince Consort didn't get onto his pedestal on the Albert Memorial until 1876; the Royal Albert Hall opened in 1871; the Midland Grand Hotel at St Pancras in 1874; and the Whitehall front of Sir Gilbert Scott's Government Offices was not completed till 1875. The Law Courts, another grand projet of the heady 1860s,

1.18 Chelsea Embankment in construction, looking east towards Chelsea Old Church and the Albert Bridge. Photograph by James Hedderly, 1873. (Historic England Archive, OP04624)

got off the ground only in 1871 and didn't finish till 1882. The Alexandra Palace, North London's answer to the Crystal Palace, had been started eight years before its completion in 1873 (fig.1.17) – and then it promptly burnt down. How old-fashioned these buildings must have looked when the scaffolding came down! New public architecture of the 1870s was thin on the ground, partly because of the anti-spending culture of Gladstone's government. An exception is Alfred Waterhouse's noble Natural History Museum (fig.1.16), erected between 1872 and 1881, but even that goes back to a submission of 1868.

In the same way, the central urban improvements of the 1870s mostly continue others planned by the Board of Works during the previous decade. The Chelsea Embankment follows on from the Victoria Embankment (fig.1.18). Clerkenwell Road picks up from the earlier Farringdon Road. Charing Cross Road and Shaftesbury Avenue likewise implement schemes suggested as far back as the 1830s and '40s. These streets have seldom won praise. Financial constraints made them the poor and narrow relations of the contemporary boulevards in Paris and other continental cities. The buildings that line them were only loosely co-ordinated. Northumberland Avenue, an offshoot of the Victoria Embankment scheme, might have been an exception; George Vulliamy, the Board of Works' architect, produced elevations for the whole length, but they were set aside in

favour of the usual eclectic jumble. At least Northumberland and Shaftesbury Avenues earned their name by acquiring trees and thus minimal boulevard status (fig 1.19).

Though all these roads were carried out in the name of easing traffic problems, many were also slum-clearance schemes. By then, the device of smashing a road through a slum in the hope that it would relieve the anguish of London's intractable housing problems was fixed and established. Everyone knew it was a crude and inadequate device, but for want of any better idea the Board of Works pressed on with it. Ever since New Oxford Street had been driven through the rookery of St Giles back in the 1840s, critics from Dickens to George Godwin of *The Builder* had pointed out that the slum-dwellers merely shifted into nearby districts, which became degraded in their turn. Successive Acts of Parliament grappled with the problem, to little avail.

From 1877, the Board of Works was obliged by law to rehouse as many people as it displaced. The favoured solution was to install those unhoused in the glum 'Five Per Cent Philanthropy' blocks of flats (so called because that was the limited dividend they were expected to pay) then becoming common (fig.1.20). But the Board was not allowed to build itself. It could only procure this sort of housing

1.19 Northumberland Avenue in 1895, looking towards Trafalgar Square. The young trees show the Metropolitan Board of Works' efforts to copy the Parisian boulevards in its later street improvements. (Collage 167782)

indirectly, by clearing sites and selling them back to private companies. The very poor could not afford the rents asked for these blocks so, as ever, they moved to adjacent areas. Meanwhile immigrants from the countryside and abroad kept crowding in and swelling the population. How to house the poor remained a headache, storing up a crisis for the next decade. All through the 1870s, the drainage and sewage situation in inner London was improving, yet mortality rates were refusing to fall. Wretched and overcrowded housing was probably the main reason.

Curiously, the only buildings that the Board of Works was empowered to erect itself were for the Metropolitan Fire Brigade. Fire stations came to the Board's door by a typical accident. Since the 1830s, a consortium of the insurance companies had paid for what passed for a London-wide fire brigade. But after its commander, James Braidwood, was killed in the Tooley Street fire of 1861, the companies refused to go on carrying the burden. So the Board was

1.20 Clarendon Buildings, Balderton Street, Mayfair. Elevation and plan of a typical 'Five Per Cent Philanthropy' block, built by the Improved Industrial Dwellings Company, 1871–2. (Drawn by Alan Fagan for the *Survey of London*)

FRONT ELEVATION TO BALDERTON STREET

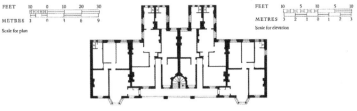

TYPICAL FLOOR PLAN

1.21 Hampstead Fire
Station, Heath Street,
in 1905. Alfred Mott,
architect, 1873.
(Collage 212309)

lumped with the responsibility, taking on Braidwood's successor, the forthright
Captain Shaw, to remodel and run the brigade from 1866. New fire stations were
urgently needed. Almost casually, the Board turned to a friend of Darwin's,
Edward Cresy junior, who was secretary to its chairman and just happened also
to be an architect. Cresy designed a large number of stations in a short time,
then died young in 1870, so fresh arrangements had to be made. Vulliamy, the
Board's superintending architect, was mostly taken up with the taxing tasks
of building control. But he now found a new assistant, Alfred Mott, to design
some extra stations. Typically for the time, these are half-Gothic, half-Italianate
(fig.1.21). All these early stations were small, so though a few survive, none
is still used as a fire station. In time Robert Pearsall took over, creating more

conspicuous and commodious stations for the Metropolitan Fire Brigade. It is with this small band of men employed within the Board of Works that the story of public-sector architecture designed and built by Britain's local authorities properly begins.

* * *

The Metropolitan Board of Works has always earned a grudging respect for the improvements it made to London's infrastructure. But no one ever much cared for it. Its members were nominated by the constituent parish vestries under the Act that created it in 1855, so it was only indirectly elected. Consequently the level of public involvement in its work was low.

That also held true for another body with a bureaucratic title that did unsung work for London throughout the 1870s, the Metropolitan Asylums Board. The MAB had been set up under legislation of 1867 in order to wrest the treatment of fever and smallpox patients, 'imbeciles' and the mentally impaired from the hands of workhouses and their Guardians, whose job it was to run the Poor Law system on a deterrence principle. These specific types of patient were now to be transferred into purpose-built hospitals – in fact 'England's First State Hospitals', to borrow the title from Gwendoline Ayers' excellent study of the MAB's work.

The legislation that set up the MAB dealt an early blow to the old ethos of laissez-faire, voluntarism and minimalism in social provision. But it was cautious. It applied only to London, where the iniquities of workhouse treatment for the infirm were perhaps most before the public eye, and to restricted categories of sickness. 'Lunatic asylums', for instance, were excluded from the provisions, and left until 1889 under the oversight of the county justices. The new MAB was to be a single central body; some of its members were directly nominated from the pre-existing central Poor Law Board, others from the various local Boards of Guardians. In fact, the early work of the MAB was hampered and braked by the Poor Law Board, to which it had to answer.

All the same it achieved a lot – and in the nick of time, as London suffered virulent smallpox epidemics in 1870–3 and again in 1876–8. The capital's first permanent smallpox hospitals, at Homerton and Stockwell, admitted patients in 1871, with Anglican nuns doing the nursing. Further fever hospitals on the approved pavilion plan opened at Deptford and Fulham in 1877. All through the decade there was a running battle at Hampstead, where the MAB earmarked the present site of the Royal Free Hospital against dogged opposition from the local bourgeoisie. A temporary infectious-diseases hospital opened there in 1870, had eventually to close under the shadow of litigation, but was finally established on a permanent basis with various constraints in 1882.

The lesson for the MAB was to locate its new hospitals well clear of prosperous suburbs. With mentally impaired patients, such mistakes were not made. Big three-storey hospitals for 1,500 patients were opened in 1870 at Leavesden in Hertfordshire and Caterham in Surrey, both far removed from built-up areas. A children's asylum with classrooms followed in 1878 at Darenth in Kent. They became the precursors of a whole ring of institutions created round the fringes of London over the last decades of the century. Now they have all been knocked down or converted into housing. We are inclined to shudder at their vaunted remoteness and self-sufficiency, isolating inmates from their families. In other respects they were generally an improvement on the workhouses that they relieved.

If we are looking for municipal idealism anywhere in the London of the 1870s, we must turn to yet another board, the School Board for London, which, following the Forster Education Act of 1870, put London's elementary schooling on a fresh and ambitious basis and controlled it until 1904.

Throughout its existence, the School Board for London was a pioneer, in advance of almost all the other school boards nationally. Unlike the MBW and the MAB, it was directly elected. Following the recent Second Reform Act of 1867

1.22 'Babies' in a ramped classroom at a board school. (Collage 178708)

the franchise was available to all male heads of households and, by an innovation that is too often forgotten, women who headed households could also vote in the triennial elections to the school boards and stand as candidates; women including Elizabeth Garrett Anderson and Annie Besant were to be active members of the London board.

'No equally powerful body will exist in England outside Parliament,' remarked *The Times* at the time of the first London school board election, 'if power be measured by influence for good or evil over masses of human beings.' The Board set a cracking pace from the start, buying sites and building energetically despite tight funding, to make up for the desperate shortage of school places in the capital; after a diligent inquiry, it planned in the first instance to provide schooling for over 100,000 children. There were nominal fees to begin with, but that didn't stop most of the working population sending their children to the new schools. There were even nurseries ('babies' rooms') in some inner-city board schools so that mothers could go to work (fig.1.22).

The board schools quickly eclipsed many small voluntary schools, ragged or religious. Most were packed from the start, taking between 600 and 1,100 pupils each in classes of 60 or more; some later schools could accommodate up to 2,000 children. The Anglicans were at first defensive about their own existing schools and hostile towards the non-denominational teaching, but mostly settled down into accepting the new schools and getting onto their management committees. Clergy, Nonconformist or Anglican but never Catholic, soon featured among the elected members of the School Board. The meetings of the Board were often fraught with controversy, particularly about religious teaching.

In architecture the School Board is a big hitter. Even now, when many of its ebullient buildings have gone or been converted to high-ceilinged flats, the hulks of the board schools loom up all over London. They were meant to impress, to rear aloft behind their high walls as proud beacons of civilisation. 'Each school stands up from its playground like a church in God's acre ringing its bell', exulted the social reformer Charles Booth. Secular churches they partly were, only with a friendlier look. It's often been observed that under E.R. Robson, the School Board's first architect, the schools picked up the avant-garde language of the Queen Anne revival, attuned to the craving for sweetness and light gaining ground in the 1870s. That is to telescope the story. The three-decker giants which the London board school usually calls to mind are creations of the 1880s and '90s, and most of them were due to the School Board architectural office under T.J. Bailey, after Robson had moved on. They were bigger and better-equipped than the schools that the Board was at first able to build.

1.23 Winchester Street School, Pentonville (now Winton School, Killick Street). Charles Barry junior, architect, 1872–3. An example of London board school architecture before E.R. Robson took charge. (*The Builder*, 21 December 1872)

1.24 Winstanley Road School, Battersea, built 1873–4. An early board school designed by E.R. Robson, now demolished. Infants' and babies' departments to the left, girls on the first floor of the main block, boys on top, all over a covered playground.

When the School Board kicked off in 1870, it was buying undersized sites because of its limited budget and trying to get buildings up in double-quick time. Having as yet no architectural staff, it plumped for competitions. Robson first makes his appearance as an adjudicator helping the Board with these competitions. After they turn out to waste time and money, Robson slips into the job of designing all the schools. Even then he continues to divide his time between the Board's offices, where Bailey was always chief assistant, and his own private bureau. As a result, the first London board schools built between about 1871 and 1874 vary. Several of these early schools survive in battered form. One example, today transformed out of recognition, is Charles Barry junior's Winchester Street School, Pentonville (fig.1.23). Even as it originally looked, one can hardly recognise what we now think of as a board school. In fact most of the competition winners were Gothic in one way or another, as indeed were most board schools built outside London during the 1870s and beyond. Robson's first London schools were Gothic too.

How then did Queen Anne insinuate itself into the board schools? The style was in the air from the early 1870s, so the competition designs were bound to be infected by it. The first fully Queen Anne school came out of the competition system in the shape of Basil Champneys' demolished Harwood Road School, Fulham. Robson then picked the style up and ran with it. Queen Anne in his hands was at first a broad church, as a school like Winstanley Road, Battersea, with its fancy stepped gables, attests (fig.1.24). It quietened down into a kind of orthodoxy after Robson went into a brief partnership with J.J. Stevenson to clear up the backlog of schools. By end of the 1870s, it had become fairly standardised.

Robson published his *School Architecture* in 1874 while in the middle of this campaign. Goodness knows how he got it out with all the press of work. It is an equivocal book, half praising what has been done and half looking over its shoulder at the bigger and better schools going up elsewhere, notably in Berlin, which Robson rushed over to check out. The schools he built in those years of urgency and economy were too cramped and tight, as the School Board soon recognised, and without school halls. Like Gothic, the Queen Anne style was adaptable to picturesque irregularity, which made it suitable for awkward sites. After Bailey took over from Robson, the sites enlarged and the architecture became more symmetrical and mechanical, also more imposing. There were always variations. Certainly the later schools, with their big central halls derived from German examples, were better educational machines.

* * *

London was expanding in the 1870s hand over fist, or rather in fits and starts. How was all that growth managed? Of planning in the modern sense of the word there was none to speak of, either physical or economic. London was still strictly laissez-faire; it had no extension or reconstruction plan of the kind that was starting to be favoured by or imposed upon continental cities. There was no active model of forethought for expanding the world's biggest city, only an accumulation of passive constraints: building regulations, sanitary by-laws and covenants imposed by landlords.

Nonetheless, in all suburban additions to the city there were shaping and determining factors. Take one example, Battersea. Here the prime determinant of urban form was the legacy of the railways. Battersea was one of several inner areas of South London brutally cut about by the so-called second railway mania of the 1860s, when the railway companies competed in bringing up their lines from the south over the Thames to new termini at Cannon Street, Blackfriars, Charing Cross and Victoria. In Battersea's case, they could do so because the suburban land they slashed through was still mostly open fields, though ripening for development. There already existed the London and South Western Railway running in south of the river towards Waterloo. In the '60s, this was joined by the

1.25 The Battersea Tangle, showing the cat's cradle of lines between Nine Elms and Clapham Junction where railways out of Waterloo and Victoria cross. Diagram of 1912, not to scale. (John Minnis)

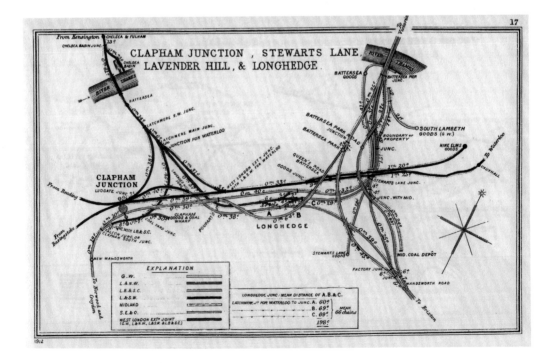

lines of the Brighton and the Chatham and Dover companies, which leapt over the earlier line to reach Victoria, leaving a set of spaghetti junctions known as the Battersea Tangle (fig.1.25). The passenger interchange between these systems grew up at Clapham Junction, famous for being Britain's busiest station – and for not being in Clapham at all.

Battersea was still reeling from this railway despoilment when it began to undergo heavy development. At that moment, proactive local government would have been helpful, but that was not London's way. Indeed, the Battersea Vestry had been downgraded under the Act that created the Metropolitan Board of Works in 1855. Powers for infrastructure in this part of south-west London had been assigned to a body called the Wandsworth Board of Works, which was superimposed upon several parishes. The idea was to provide a better co-ordinated service for drainage, road layout and lighting than a local vestry could offer. That worked well enough. But it was a wholly passive approach; the Wandsworth Board merely decided whether development proposals conformed with the various regulations and had no forward-looking policies. It was also irresponsive to local needs and sentiments. As Battersea's population doubled in the 1870s (54,000 in 1871; 109,000 in 1881), the Wandsworth Board became the butt of frustration and anger. This virtually new town wanted to manage its own destiny. That finally happened in 1887, when by a special Act of Parliament Battersea escaped the Wandsworth Board and resumed full vestry powers of its own. This back history helps explain why Battersea took to radicalism and socialism in the last years of the century.

By the 1870s industry had already taken over a lot of Battersea's river frontage and was creeping inland. New housing areas for workers or commuters had to be tucked awkwardly between the railway lines and factories, often on ill-drained land. The great sewerage schemes of the 1860s made some difference but not enough, so that many of the houses built on low-lying sites nearer the Thames soon became sub-standard and have since been demolished.

All this was an inhibition to decent planning or architecture in Battersea. The outstanding exception was the Shaftesbury Park Estate off Lavender Hill. This large enclave of little two-storey terrace houses was built in the 1870s by the Artizans', Labourers', and General Dwellings Company, the only 'Five Per Cent Philanthropy' company to specialise in suburban housing on a big scale. Another such estate, not much smaller, was built at Queen's Park off the Harrow Road in north-west London. Promoted at first as 'the workmen's city', Shaftesbury Park (figs 1.26, 1.27) has survived well. Less than a third of its houses were multi-occupied in its early years – a sure sign of success. It aimed to be 'respectable'.

1.26 (above) Shaftesbury Park, Battersea. Bird's eye view of the Artizans', Labourers', and General Dwellings Company Estate. (*The Graphic*, 28 November 1874)

1.27 (left) Shaftesbury Park, Battersea. Typical houses of the 1870s in Birley Street and Eversleigh Road.

1.28 (above right) 50–68 Onslow Gardens, South Kensington. Late Italianate houses built by the developer and builder C.J. Freake, 1873–5.

1.29, 1.30 (right) 19–31 De Vere Gardens, Kensington. General view and detail.

There were evening classes, flower shows and cottage-garden competitions, a co-operative shop but no licensed premises. The population came not from the gravely poor but from 'the upper levels of the working class or the lower middle class'. Although some of them worked in the local factories or train depots, Shaftesbury Park had plenty of commuters to central London. 'Many fulfilled lowly duties for official bodies such as government departments, law courts, the military and the British Museum.' Despite the 'workmen's city' name, this then was a suburb for clerks as much as industrial workers.

Despite the havoc wreaked by the railways, Battersea was lucky enough to be endowed with three great open spaces whose edges had already attracted some high-class commuters and might be expected to attract more. Battersea Park, created under the auspices of the Crown, went back to the 1840s. Probably because it was on low-lying ground too close to the river, the surrounding housing development that had been planned to pay for it hung fire till the flat-building decades of the 1880s and '90s. The other two open spaces, Clapham and Wandsworth Commons, occupied higher and healthier land on Battersea's fringes. Both belonged to the ancient commons with which London's environs had once been plenteously endowed. Over the previous century, they had been steadily eaten away by landlords, villa-builders, speculators, squatters and railways. Wandsworth Common, for instance, had lost almost half its acreage since the 1780s.

The struggle to secure what was left of these prized assets, the so-called lungs of the metropolis, had long been entangled in legal rights and technicalities. The breakthrough came only after George Shaw Lefevre founded the Commons Preservation Society – the first modern amenity society – in 1865. That marked the start of a wider movement to safeguard and open up public access to unbuilt spaces, small and large, not least closed inner-city churchyards, in which the sisters Octavia and Miranda Hill played a notable part during the 1870s. For London's commons, an Act of 1866 laid the groundwork. As a result, some of the greatest of them were vested in the Metropolitan Board of Works – Hampstead Heath (in Michael Thompson's words 'one of the hottest metropolitan potatoes of the century') after an epic struggle in 1870–1, Clapham Common in 1877, Wandsworth Common not until 1887. After similar campaigns Wimbledon Common passed to a board of conservators in 1871, Epping Forest to the City of London's care in 1878. From scruffy areas for foraging and putting out animals to pasture, the surviving London commons turned into places primarily for recreation – safe at least by day, and on the whole competently managed.

* * *

Let's turn now to a different kind of housing. Tall, up-and-down dwellings jammed together in rows, otherwise 'terraces', had hogged the high end of the London market for two centuries. We usually think of housing of this type as generated and governed by the 'Great Estates' that had long dominated the growth of the West End, Belgravia and beyond. On that model, the lines of development were laid down by a powerful freeholder and his agents: chiefly a surveyor, who marked out the plots, assigned them to builders and tried to ensure uniformity of frontage, and a lawyer, who settled the terms of the lease (by the 1870s, generally for 80 or 99 years) and the covenants to be observed – all with a view to maintaining the estate's long-term value on its 'reversion' to the freeholder.

For a tissue of reasons, no new Great Estates of the old and enduring London type came into being after 1870. Large tracts of suburban land were still however sometimes developed by a single freeholder or big builder. Outstanding examples include the builder Edward Yates, who owned 2,345 houses by the end of his career, erected on both freehold and leasehold property in Walworth and Camberwell; and Alfred Heaver, with an estimated tally of over 4,000 houses built in pockets all over south-west London, ranging from Clapham to Earlsfield. Bigger still was Archibald Cameron Corbett, who laid out swathes of East London from the late 1870s – we shall meet him later in Ilford.

But proprietors of this kind seldom exercised absolute long-term control over the streets and houses they built. Changes in housing finance had something to do with this. The leasehold system was an intricate mechanism dependent on low levels of capital investment but a lot of borrowed money at the time of building. Small investors, particularly widows and single women, put their savings into mortgages on leasehold property via solicitors. This now dwindled away, as other types of investment became more available and building societies took over the mortgage market. Increasingly, too, some householders were pressing to buy the freeholds of their houses where they could. Other factors were the sheer number of new estates, large or small, often less personally managed, and greater variation in the types of dwellings on offer. These changes made the old dynastic aspirations impossible.

That left the existing great landowners of the West End and Bloomsbury, the likes of the Bedford, Grosvenor, Portland and Portman Estates, in a unique situation. So successfully did they maintain and even strengthen their position from this time that they have survived to this day, little reduced in reach or power. The Grosvenors, for instance, undertook a spate of rebuilding when leases expired on their Mayfair estate, which saw the wealth and public standing of its owner from the 1870s, the first Duke of Westminster, far exceed that of his country-squire ancestors who had presided over its first development. In Marylebone, updating the even larger Portland Estate was less personal but just as effective. Very few sales of freeholds took place, and the Portland dynasty's authority was confirmed by the building of an estate office in 1882 from which its officials and rent collectors were supposed to work instead of the previous decentralised system. The Bedford Estate had bigger problems, as Bloomsbury lost caste and its outlying districts deteriorated. Far from losing its grip, however, the Estate 'became ever more dictatorial in renewing leases and stipulating the uses to which buildings could and could not be put', according to Simon Jenkins.

Leaseholders, especially shopkeepers, often resented this system, as the prosperity they brought to an area through their labours was channelled back to the freeholder in the increased value of his land, and then boomeranged back on them in the shape of higher rents when leases were renewed. This resentment began to be articulated in the 1880s, at the time of the social disturbances chronicled in the next chapter. A Commons committee looked into all this in 1887, and the journalist Frank Banfield followed up with a set of articles collected into a book, *The Great Landlords of London*. Banfield lashed the whole leasehold system and concluded that 'the power possessed by the agents of the ground landlords is an anachronism, as to-day it exists divorced from responsibility to public opinion'. But as yet little changed.

Opulent Kensington is the best place to study the last hurrah of London's high-class terrace housing. Onslow Gardens is a classic piece of old-style London estate development. Built on land belonging to the competently run Smith's Charity Estate, it stretches in date from about 1863 to 1878, prolonging a scheme started back in the 1840s. So it represents continuity and conservatism. But the houses of the 1870s (fig.1.28) are a good deal bigger than the Estate's earlier ones, running to as many as six tiring storeys high (no passenger lifts yet). That means different proportions both for the elevations and for the street scene as a whole. The materials have also become more 'real' in Victorian terms. Stucco has receded in favour of hard yellow brick, and there is less attempt to disguise the roof.

For a contrast in style of development if not in architecture we can turn to De Vere Gardens, started just after Baron Grant's Kensington House close by. Occupying a small freehold sold in 1875 to a surveyor and a builder, it consists of a single canyon-like street. The note of hardness and realism sounds louder here and the look is a shade more eclectic (figs 1.29, 1.30). Bare granite columns to the porticos and triplets of Italianate windows jostle with French-style balconies. There is something determined but heartless about such houses. Too often they come in long, monotonous street-runs instead of facing squares or gardens. The 'gardens' in De Vere Gardens is a lie – there are no gardens, front or back. The houses are now so gargantuan that they swallow up the whole plot.

De Vere Gardens did not do well, taking years to fill up. Before the end of the 1870s, flats were being built on the vacant plots instead (Henry James took one for a time) and soon vacant properties were being converted into flats or even hotels, still clinging to the look of individual houses. The two sets of mews, tucked in at the end of the development, were 'always in excess of the residents' needs'. By a space-saving device borrowed from industrial stabling in central London, they were planned on two storeys, coach-houses below and stalls above, reached by a horse-ramp. They limped on into the age of motorisation. Then one of the mews was converted into bijou cottages, more eligible and convenient than the ponderous old houses.

Private stabling was on its way out in London by the 1870s. In Cadogan Square and some other posh developments, the preferred Georgian arrangement of stabling directly behind the houses lingered on. But most Victorians were keen to keep the smells and noise at a distance, in separate blocks of stabling at arm's length from the houses. In either case, stabling was tiresome to maintain and difficult to supervise. As Michael Thompson put it in a memorable lecture, 'Horses are hard work'. The proportion of stabling to high-class houses, never one to one, was falling all through the Victorian reign. Onslow Square and Onslow Gardens provided less stabling than the earlier squares of Belgravia, and there was less again at De Vere Gardens. In another Kensington development of the period, the ratio was about one set of stabling to four houses; in cheaper suburbs it would have been lower. In the better districts a servant could always be sent out to hire a cab or make a regular arrangement with one of the jobmasters who filled up the empty accommodation in the mews. Nor, so long as they could travel first class, did any but the grandest householders disdain the Underground, accessible at South Kensington, Gloucester Road and High Street Kensington from 1868, and at Earl's Court from 1871.

* * *

By 1870 the Classical Italianate idiom was worn out as a style for terrace houses; something fresh was sorely needed. Gothic had seldom found favour for town-houses, but there had been experiments in French variants of Classicism, usually in the form of the tall, mansard-roofed style called Second Empire. Napoleon III's extensions to the Louvre in the 1850s had rekindled interest in reviving this seventeenth-century French idiom. Second Empire first hit London in a spate of fashionable large hotels, notably station hotels. An ebullient example was the Grosvenor Hotel outside Victoria, opened in 1862 to designs by James Knowles junior – who was fond of French styles, as Kensington House confirmed. Complementing the Grosvenor are the nearby blocks of Grosvenor Gardens, London's first major housing development in the Second Empire manner, begun soon after the hotel.

Had Napoleon III's reign carried on in its somewhat tawdry glory, London might have seen more of this manner. But after his abject defeat at Prussian hands in 1870, followed by the bloodiness and bitterness of the Commune, Paris and France fell out of architectural favour. In this respect architecture differs from art. There had been close relations between French and English painters during the Second Empire, and many émigré artists came to London to escape the Commune. Afterwards the fashion for French painting and sculpture (the latter still streets ahead of its English counterpart) persisted. In architecture the same interchange was lacking. Some recovery of interest took place after 1878, when France held another of its international exhibitions and George Augustus Sala wrote a bouncy book about it called *Paris Herself Again*. All the same, Paris ceased to be an architectural paradigm until almost 1900, leaving the field open for the rest of the century to the Englishness of English architecture.

The mansarded style did, it is true, enjoy a few late outings in Kensington during the 1870s. An example is Redcliffe Square, designed by George Godwin of *The Builder* and his brother Henry (fig.1.33). Apart from a few knobs and twiddles

1.31 Redcliffe Mansions, 29–45 Redcliffe Square, Kensington. George and Henry Godwin, architects, 1871. In Redcliffe Square and elsewhere, Second Empire roofs and ornament are clamped on to the London terrace house. (*The Builder*, 11 February 1871)

1.32 Cornwall House and Garden House, Cornwall Gardens, Kensington. James Trant Smith, architect, for William Willett, builder, 1877–8. (Kensington Libraries)

and a certain angularity, it is not so different from De Vere Gardens and it got a poor press. Another effort came from the emerging building firm of the two William Willetts, father and son, on the fag end of a development in Cornwall Gardens. Along the edges, they carried on the tired Italian terrace idiom, but in the centre the Willetts in 1877–9 put up six socking French-style mansions designed by James Trant Smith as semi-detacheds on the grandest scale, with 'mod cons' – billiard rooms, marble floors, electric bells, speaking tubes between all the rooms and wedding-cake frills on the outside. Though far from great architecture, they had verve. These houses didn't do well; an early photograph (fig.1.32) betrays a forlorn 'to let or sell' notice, with the Willett office sign in the background. Four of the six were soon converted to flats.

From the mid-1870s, the home-grown Queen Anne style started to supplant these clumsy Gallicisms in the high-class domestic market. It arose out of attempts

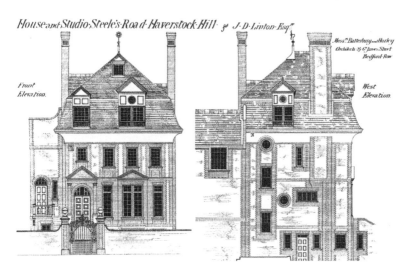

House and Studio, Steele's Road, Haverstock Hill. for J. D. Linton Esq.

Messrs Batterbury and Huxley
Orchitects 15 & 6 James Street
Bedford Row

Front
Elevation

West
Elevation

1.33 Studio houses for Charles Johnson (left) and J.D. Linton (right), 35 and 36 Steele's Road, Haverstock Hill. Batterbury and Huxley, architects, 1875. (Geoff Brandwood)

1.34 Elevations and plan of studio house for the watercolour painter J.D. Linton, 36 Steele's Road, Haverstock Hill. Batterbury and Huxley, architects, 1875. (*Building News*, 9 February 1877)

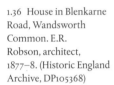

1.35 Houses in Hampstead Hill Gardens. Batterbury and Huxley, architects, late 1870s. (Geoff Brandwood)

1.36 House in Blenkarne Road, Wandsworth Common. E.R. Robson, architect, 1877–8. (Historic England Archive, DP105368)

to reform and refresh not the terrace house but the London suburban villa. This house-type had a history reaching far back and, as is the way with successful things, going progressively down market. The first step down the slippery slope had been to split the villa in two, creating the semi-detached house. By the mid-century, the hackneyed term had lost any vestige of superiority. So-called villas, singly or in pairs, had sprung up in every conceivable bastard or degraded style all over the suburbs – a trend explored in an essay of John Summerson's with a blend of curiosity and fastidious distaste. Complete London streets had purloined the villa name, even when the best they could boast were runs of close-knit semi-detacheds. It was high time to drop the term and restore verve and grace to groups of independent houses.

Belsize Park, on the ascent towards Hampstead, is a good place to witness the birth of Queen Anne out of the ruck of domestic styles. From the time of its first development, this amenable suburb had been large-scale semi-detached territory, ranging from the pretty Eton Villas of the 1840s to Belsize Park Gardens of the 1860s, where the pompous stuccoed pairs are divided by only the meanest sliver of space. All this broke down quite suddenly and sharply after 1870, following the bankruptcy of a major builder.

The honour for making the change fell to two small Belsize Park developments designed by the obscure partnership of Batterbury and Huxley. The first cluster of these independent houses, started in 1872, is in Steele's Road. Here the new manner is born and matures before our eyes, from a bargeboarded house that might be called Gothic to others sporting all the quaint new Queen Anne appurtenances – gables, covings and white sash windows (figs 1.33, 1.34). Artists were the main clients for these houses, which incorporate studios at the back. Though some of them were initially called villas, they begin to draw away from the world conjured up by that pretentious name. Up the hill and a year or two on in Hampstead Hill Gardens, the architecture has already arrived at something resembling the genuine Queen Anne style of the early eighteenth century, or even the Georgian housing that followed (fig.1.35). It is as if a whole century of English house-styles is being avidly and rapidly recapitulated.

This new domestic style or bag of styles is hard to pin down or cage. Yet it feels right for the loosening-up London of the 1870s. We can call it Queen Anne if we like, but as with all worthwhile art movements the name is just a handle. Further up the hill in Redington Road, Hampstead, is a quiet semi-detached pair by Philip Webb of the same years. They are more thoughtful than Batterbury and Huxley's inventions, yet they belong to the same moment. Or there's the flamboyant house in Ellerdale Road, near Hampstead parish church, that Norman Shaw built for

1.37 Studio houses in Tite Street, Chelsea, by R.W. Edis, foreground, and E.W. Godwin, in distance. (Historic England Archive, BL03143)

himself, in another idiom again. Down at Wandsworth Common, Robson of School Board fame designed a small group of 'villas', two with Queen Anne gables, a third half-timbered, a fourth with bow windows and parapets (fig.1.36). Only red brickwork and tall chimneys draw all these houses together – plus an elusive quality of Englishness.

Such houses breathe an optimism and individualism new to English architecture. Freedom is the best word for it. The phrase 'free style' is sometimes used about the 1890s, but it fits the 1870s better. It's notable that many of the early showpieces of the Queen Anne movement – Batterbury and Huxley's in Belsize Park, Shaw's in Kensington and E.W. Godwin's and R.W. Edis's in Chelsea (fig.1.37)

– were studio houses. The artists who commissioned them were of unequal fame and merit. But such by now was the appetite for art that a wide range of artists could hope to earn well and live well by it, and with a new freedom of lifestyle. Reynolds and Lawrence, Turner and Constable, had all had their own studios, sometimes highly personal but tucked away from sight. Now art and artists were in the broader public realm. Before the 1870s were done, speculative groups of Queen Anne studios were even being built in Belsize Park and Kensington, on sites where stables had first been planned.

Queen Anne may have started out as just one of a jumble of ideas that were being tried out at a directionless moment in urban architecture but by the end of the 1870s it had triumphed. This victory can be seen in the shift of the board-school production line from a medley of styles to Queen Anne. It can be traced too in a change of tack among up-and-coming London architects. One such was Ernest George, who began his career toying with ornamental variants of Gothic, manifest for instance in a handsome house in Stratton Street, Mayfair. Very soon and only a few streets further north, he gave the Queen Anne style its first major commercial outing when he rebuilt the premises of the china merchants Thomas Goode and Co. (fig.1.38). George never looked back.

1.38 Premises for Thomas Goode and Co., china merchants, South Audley Street, Mayfair. Ernest George and Peto, architects, 1875–6. (Martin Charles)

1.39, 1.40 Studio house for Marcus Stone, Melbury Road, Kensington, front and back. R. Norman Shaw, architect, 1875–6. (Martin Charles)

1.41 New Zealand
Chambers, Leadenhall
Street, City of London.
An attempt to
romanticise the City's
commercial architecture.
Perspective exhibited
by Norman Shaw at the
Royal Academy, 1873.
(Royal Academy)

It is Norman Shaw who best represents the currents at work in smarter London
houses during the budding of the Queen Anne movement – its changefulness and
elasticity, its see-sawing between old and new, its whiff of amorality and mischief,
its easiness yet uneasiness, its aura of freedom, hope and fun. Shaw is at the height
of his inventiveness in the 1870s. His dashing perspectives steal the architectural
show at the Royal Academy's annual exhibitions. They are then disseminated

in the building press, reproduced with a fineness of line made feasible by the new photolithography. Usually they illustrate his 'Old English' country houses. Yet Shaw's most original architecture is built in London. In Holland Park, for instance, he designs two studio houses in Melbury Road (figs 1.39, 1.40) for the painters Marcus Stone and Luke Fildes, high-earning artists of the type who held on at the Academy when the avant-garde was deserting to the Grosvenor. They are as bold as William Burges's robustly Gothic castle-home in the same road or Godwin's studio houses for the aesthetes of Chelsea, and more flexible and wayward than either. Architecture might go anywhere from here.

In the 1870s, Shaw seems capable of dazzling in almost any building type or style. Several experiments and lines of development are going on in his work simultaneously. Sometimes they do not come off, like his grand Lowther Lodge on Kensington Gore, full of fizz and tricks yet restless and contrived. Then there are the historical character portraits. The most famous of Shaw's London buildings in its day was New Zealand Chambers in Leadenhall Street (fig.1.41), no longer with us because it was blitzed in 1941. Here he teased and goaded the City of London by harking back to its old timber architecture, before the Great Fire, in a piece of play-acting based on a rare survival – Sir Paul Pindar's house in Bishopsgate. It could never have been a model for modern building in the City – timber and plaster fronts were forbidden by the building regulations – so Shaw had to cheat and compromise. But New Zealand Chambers proffered an implicit challenge and reproach, hinting that Jacobean merchant-life was more honourable and English than the world of the Melmottes. As a sally in nostalgic criticism, it sits alongside *The Way We Live Now*.

Another character portrait did catch on: dressing up the London merchant as a Dutch or Flemish burgher. That was to lead the Queen Anne movement down the primrose path to the Low Countries. It took off particularly in Chelsea. Along the new Chelsea Embankment, Shaw and some other architects gave their exuberant houses the image of a town quay on a Dutch canal. Away from the river on one side of Cadogan Square, houses with extravagant gables by Shaw and Ernest George recreated the jostling emulation of set-pieces such as the Grand Place in Brussels. In lesser hands this style soon got onto the production line and lost its precious individuality, as a glance at the other three sides of Cadogan Square confirms.

Bedford Park, in London's outer western suburbs, is the character portrait that best stands for the scent of freedom that came with the Queen Anne style. The place still commands great local affection and loyalty. That is partly because of the architectural charm Shaw endowed it with, but there is more to Bedford

1.42 Semi-detached
houses in The Avenue,
Bedford Park, 1878.
In the foreground, an
early pair by Norman
Shaw; to the left, houses
designed by Coe and
Robinson. (Bedford
Lemere photograph in
Francis Loeb Library,
Harvard Graduate School
of Design)

Park than that. It also represents a step forward in the making of better-looking middle-class suburbs imbued with a community spirit.

Jonathan Carr, the promoter and freeholder of Bedford Park, could have been a Trollope creation. As idealists often are, Carr was plausible but risk-taking. He was active as a Radical Liberal at a time when Radicalism still had an identity and a vigour of its own on the left wing of the Liberal Party and had yet to be eclipsed by socialism. He had political ambitions, which he would have followed up if his finances had not gone drastically wrong. So Bedford Park is more accurately a radical suburb than a pioneer garden suburb, as it is often anachronistically termed.

Carr believed in personal freedom. That spirit, remote from the mood and management of the Great Estates, is the crucial feature about Bedford Park. Started on land next to Turnham Green Station acquired by Carr's father-in-law, it looked at first as if it would be just another commuter suburb for the middle classes, who leased or rented houses in the usual way. Like most developments of the 1870s, it was not fully planned or conceived from the start. The houses were to be up to date, architect-designed, and without the chilly damp basements that caused so much domestic misery. So far, all so good but not perhaps so special. Then, as if by magic, the railway suburb turned into a community where residents were treated as equals and could meet one another and 'the promoter' socially in the club, at church or at the co-operative stores. Between about 1877 and 1882, Carr bravely realised that vision, withstanding outside suspicion and mockery. It receded after he entangled himself in other developments and failed. But the buildings are mostly still there, and in their innocent good cheer embody a memory of those first libertarian hopes.

1.43 Final version of
Shaw's detached-house
designs for Bedford Park.
(Martin Charles)

Carr was not too fussy about who designed the houses at Bedford Park, nor was he overkeen about paying them. But he wanted a name to attract buyers, and in 1877, when his first choice, E.W. Godwin, failed to live up to expectations, Shaw's was the most marketable in London for domestic architecture. The core of the job was designing adaptable house-types. That, not planning street layouts, was what an architect was expected to do for speculative estate development. Shaw took some pains with the semi-detached type, designing three versions to improve and economise on the plans. The elevations show him balancing between the Queen Anne style he used in London and the Old English he preferred for the countryside (figs 1.42, 1.43).

If the houses of Bedford Park invite any allusion, it is to the freeborn Englishman from the era of the Glorious Revolution, as portrayed in the pages of Macaulay or the essays of Addison and Steele. Not that either Carr or Shaw tried

1.44 The Bedford Park Club with the Tower House behind, 1881. (Historic England Archive, BB65/00614)

1.45 Bedford Park in 1881 looking along Bath Road, with the stores and the church. (Historic England Archive, BL02832)

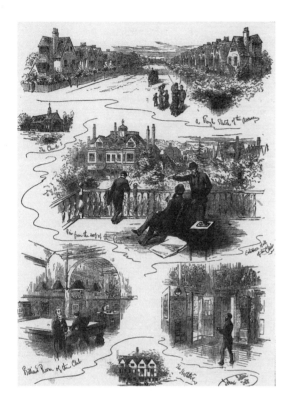

1.46 Sketches of Bedford Park by John Jellicoe. *Above*: The Avenue; centre, the church and the Tower House from the club roof; *Below*: the club and the 'hostelry'. (*Illustrated Sporting and Dramatic News*, 27 September 1879)

to press so far-fetched an image on the suburb. It was just in the air to pick up, if you wished; and a few perceptive critics did so. On top of that came a tinge of Aestheticism, perhaps due in the first place to the influence of Jonathan Carr's younger brother J. Comyns Carr, the brains behind the Grosvenor Gallery. But it was not predominant. Though some second-rank artists lived in Bedford Park, most of its early heads of household were in trade.

Shaw designed four special buildings during his involvement with Bedford Park – the church; the Tabard Inn; Jonathan Carr's own home, the Tower House; and the club that was the centre of social life, quite different from some bare tenants' hall (figs 1.44, 1.45). A fifth, the art school, was built after Shaw had become disillusioned with Carr (he was supposed to get £5 per house but probably never did). The art school and the Tower House have gone, and the club has been compromised. All we have left at the heart of Shaw's character-sketch (fig.1.46) is the group of inn, store and church near the station. The Tabard looks like a cross between a homely village pub and the temperance inns into which reformers were trying to lure the drinkers of the day. The church is equally equivocal. It's Gothic, traditional and ecclesiological – sort of; yet it's also free, relaxed and aesthetic – sort of. It faces both ways, not without levity. We know the church was intended to tease, because Shaw later said so to his admirer Hermann Muthesius, German author of pioneering books on English architecture: 'Of course that was a sort of joke to make the proper Gothic man angry – and it did make him very angry.'

Where did Jonathan Carr go to after Bedford Park? The answer takes us back to Kensington House. Baron Grant's French monstrosity was razed, and on its site Carr promoted the houses of Kensington Court. This time his architect was not Shaw, who wanted no more to do with him, but another of the Queen Anne pioneers, J.J. Stevenson. Here was Queen Anne with a difference. Each house had hydraulic lifts; a hire company provided plants on the forecourts and balconies; and soon electric light was installed. After Carr failed, flats came. Kensington Court belongs to the London of the 1880s.

2

London in the 1880s

On 14 March 1883, Karl Marx died at 41 Maitland Park Road, Haverstock Hill, the London house where he had lived the longest (fig.2.1). His last years were beset by health and family troubles. Since the first book of *Das Kapital* came out in 1867, he had been labouring on with the later volumes amid interruptions. Marx was much visited by comrades, mainly German and Russian, and he pamphleteered about political developments in both countries – he was cheered, for instance, by the assassination of Tsar Alexander II in 1881. He took less interest in England and its politics.

Marx was away from home a lot. Two of his three daughters were married to French socialists, Laura to Paul Lafargue and Jenny to Charles Longuet. Both men had fled to London after the Paris Commune, but returned in the easier French political climate of the 1880s. Marx and his wife, also Jenny, were close to the Longuets and good grandparents, staying with them outside Paris whenever they could. But Marx was troubled by heart problems and his wife had cancer. She came back from Paris to Haverstock Hill in the summer of 1881 and died after months of pain in December. She was the first to be buried in the famous grave in Highgate Cemetery (fig.2.2). Karl went off to the Isle of Wight with Eleanor, his favourite daughter, and on to Paris and Algiers for his health. He was hardly in London during 1882. Then, early the next year, Jenny Longuet died in Paris of bladder cancer. This further blow devastated Marx; he followed his daughter two months later. So there was a second burial at Highgate, this time with about a dozen family and comrades present. Despite some declamations at the graveside, few Londoners took much notice. Only a handful of English socialists, economists and intellectuals knew about Marx's great work. He had attracted

2.1 41 Maitland Park
Road, Haverstock Hill.
Karl Marx's last home,
now demolished. The
photo dates from 1935,
when the LCC plaque was
installed. It was twice
vandalised and never
replaced. (Collage 110217)

attention as a firebrand at the time of
the Paris Commune; since then his star
seemed to have faded.

* * *

Yet strangely, from the moment of
Marx's death the political temperature
in England, and London in particular,
started to rise. Demonstrations,
agitations and riots followed, bringing
London in the 1880s closer to revolution
than it had been for seventy years,
or has been since. By the end of the
decade, reforms had done something to
appease the protests. But the legacy of
these troubled years lived on.

Marx had little to do with all this.
Until the late 1880s, the first book
of *Das Kapital* was available only in
German, Russian or French. Only a
handful of English readers had a go
at it during Marx's lifetime. Just one of these comes centrally into the story of
the disturbances of the 1880s. That was Henry Mayers Hyndman, businessman,
cricketer, imperialist, anti-Semite (both tricky positions for an admirer of Marx),
founder of the Social Democratic Federation, arguably the first British Marxist,
certainly the first British champagne socialist.

Hyndman (fig.2.3) was a queer bundle of cleverness, obstinacy and egotism.
Nobody liked him much, but they had to admit he had courage. The joke was
that he turned revolutionary socialist because he didn't get into the first eleven at
Cambridge. After bumming around the world, Hyndman came back in the 1870s
and turned to political journalism, writing especially for the *Pall Mall Gazette*.
Like many Radicals he loathed the way in which Gladstone played on Christian
sympathies over the so-called Bulgarian atrocities, siding with autocratic Russia
against the Ottoman Empire and so levering himself back into power in 1880.
Someone gave Hyndman a copy of the first volume of *Das Kapital* in French to read
on a boat trip to the States. He came back converted, got in touch with Marx and
bugged him for a few months. Hyndman calls him 'a powerful, shaggy, untamed

old man, ready, not to say eager to enter into conflict and rather suspicious himself of immediate attack'. After a while Marx got fed up with him and broke off relations, but not before Hyndman had published an article on 1 January 1881 in the literary magazine *Nineteenth Century* entitled 'The Dawn of a Revolutionary Epoch'. Here is an extract.

2.2 Marx's grave, Highgate Cemetery. The inscription from the original grave, which was elsewhere in the cemetery, has been incorporated in the Laurence Bradshaw monument of 1956.

> At a period such as ours anything may happen ... Religious sanctions are shaken in every country, political institutions are themselves in a state of fusion ... the growing knowledge and power of the masses leads them to consider more and more seriously the strange inequalities of our existing arrangements, the spread of ideas from one centre to another is so rapid as almost to defy calculation. Can it be said then that we are safe for any length of time from the shock of one of those convulsions which may change the whole social prospect? ... The old days of aristocracy and class privileges are passing away fast; we have to consider now how to deal with the growing democratic influence, so that we may benefit by the experience of others. This can only be done by a steady determination at the outset to satisfy the needs and gratify the reasonable ambition of all.

2.3 Henry Mayers
Hyndman in mid-life,
probably in the 1890s.
(Wikipedia)

Compared, say, to the old revolutionary outbursts of Shelley, this is tame stuff. Yet they were the words of someone who was ready to organise. There was little English socialism at the time, and certainly no socialist party. The Radicals, intellectually the disciples of John Stuart Mill, came closest. They were mostly middle-class and linked to the Liberal Party, though they had their own London working men's clubs. At the working-class level, Chartism had died long ago but its struggle lingered in the memory. The trade union movement was only for skilled artisans; and though the franchise had been extended in 1867 to all male householders in boroughs, that was still less than half the adult male population.

So little sense of direction did Hyndman have that he went to get advice not just from Marx but also from another grand old man, Disraeli. William Morris, whose political roots lay in a romantic, Ruskinian Toryism, was beginning to think along similar lines, but he was a year or two behind Hyndman, who followed up his words with deeds. In June 1881, he published a little book called *England for All*, then set up his Democratic Federation in November that year. This was renamed the Social Democratic Federation, or SDF, in 1884, when a weekly magazine, *Justice*, was launched. Morris had thrown in his lot with Hyndman early in 1882, and the young George Bernard Shaw also joined. There was a moment when the three of them could be found selling *Justice* on London street corners, Hyndman wearing his top hat.

So by the time Marx died there was the faintest stirring of socialist organisation. Then things went wrong. Hyndman liked to control things, enjoyed hobnobbing with grand people, had little time for trade unions and hoped to get into Parliament. His socialism was really about political theory and economics, not the plight of the working classes. Morris, more emotional, cared about comradeship, propaganda and culture. In 1884, as the movement was taking off, came an acrimonious split; Morris and his friends seceded to found the Socialist League (fig.2.4), which tends to get the better press today. Yet the League proved less sustainable than the Federation, so that Morris came back to the 'right but repulsive' SDF for the last years of his life. All the same, during the great years of London agitations, 1885–9, there were two rival socialist organisations vying for the loyalty of the working classes and feuding behind a public veneer of unity.

One more figure should be introduced before we come on to the disturbances themselves. That is an American, Henry George (fig.2.5). In 1879, George published *Progress and Poverty*, which ascribed the massive inequalities of wealth and poverty to the monopoly of land. His one answer to all the great social questions was – tax the land, so as to release its wealth to the rest of the community. He was neither a socialist nor a specially deep thinker, but he was a persuasive speaker

2.4 William Morris and the Hammersmith Branch of the Socialist League, 1888. (Martin Stott)

and writer in the Victorian preaching mode: Hyndman said that George had a 'bump of reverence . . . of cathedral proportions'.

Henry George first became involved with Britain because of the festering Irish question, at its most poisonous in the early 1880s. Control of the land was at the heart of Irish politics. The agitations of the Irish National Land League led to a series of agrarian outrages, then to the Coercion Act which suspended habeas corpus in Ireland, and then to the shocking Phoenix Park murders in 1882, when the newly appointed Irish Secretary, Lord Frederick Cavendish, was assassinated, alarming England.

George was in London at the time, and got himself briefly arrested on a visit to Ireland soon afterwards. The English edition of *Progress and Poverty* sold an amazing 100,000 copies, and when George addressed the Land Nationalisation Society in London he was received with adulation. Bernard Shaw was there, and remembered:

He spoke of Liberty, Justice, Truth, Natural Law and other strange eighteenth-century superstitions . . . [he] explained with great simplicity and serenity the views of the Creator, who had gone completely out of fashion in London in the previous decade and had not been heard of since. I noticed that he was a born orator, and that he had small plump and pretty hands . . . When I was thus swept into the great Socialist revival of 1883, I found that five-sixths of those who were swept in with me had been converted by Henry George.

For a moment Hyndman hoped to join up with George, but after the rapturous welcome offered to the latter by thousands when he came back to London in January 1884, it grew clear that Hyndman's one-track doctrines were too narrow. His star slowly faded, though he continued to have a following among English land reformers such as Ebenezer Howard.

2.5 Henry George in the mid-1880s. (Wikimedia Commons, New York Public Library)

* * *

Thus far we have heard only about the few middle-class leaders of Shaw's 'great Socialist revival of 1883'. One could add in another middle-class initiative, the Fabian Society, founded at the start of the following year to further inform debate about social conditions and economics, with Shaw's lively participation. But political movements get nowhere without a body of adherents – in this case those working-class people for whom the Bulgarian or even the Irish question came second to their own daily condition and interests.

It was Hyndman's achievement to draw into his Democratic Federation a new set of working-class leaders and trade unionists, organised, energetic and better educated than the Chartist generation: men like Tom Mann, vegetarian and teetotaller, the dockers' leader in their great strike of 1889; Harry Quelch, originally a packer in a City warehouse; the charismatic John Burns, later an MP and cabinet minister; and others. Most were skilled workers, members of the so-called labour aristocracy – engineers, carpenters and the like. But the SDF did not disdain the unskilled and the jobless, who helped swell its rank and file at a moment when the scourge of unemployment and the plight of the poorest were at the forefront of discontent.

The bright star among this new brand of working-class militants was John Burns (fig.2.6). A Scottish railwayman's son from Battersea, Burns had a good elementary education at a church school, where he acquired a lifelong love of books. He went into the engineering trades, became radicalised by an exile from the Paris Commune, and in 1878 at the age of nineteen earned his first arrest for speaking at a rally on Clapham Common. Outdoor rallies in the parks or outside factory and dock gates were a crucial tool in the socialist armoury during the 1880s. Burns soon joined the SDF and became the life and soul of the Battersea branch, one of the party's strongest.

Though the SDF was meant to be a national political party, it was very London-centred. It had 24 branches there in 1887 but few in the provinces, Lancashire apart. That proved its Achilles heel. The Independent Labour Party, rooted in the industrial districts of the North and linked to Nonconformist traditions of faith and steady behaviour, grew to prominence in the 1890s. In parallel, the SDF, rationalistic and revolutionary in character, dwindled away. All the same, it was the SDF that led the dramatic eruption of working-class agitation in London, starting with the Trafalgar Square clashes of 1886–7. These events have never quite been effaced from popular memory, and their story is still worth retelling. As always with riots, there are many versions of what happened and why.

2.6 John Burns in the workshop of J.G. Lorrain, electrical engineer, 1888. (Wandsworth Local History Library)

Since Chartist days there had been a tradition of demonstration in Trafalgar Square, as the closest open space to government offices in Whitehall (Parliament Square didn't then exist in its modern form). Wellington had succeeded in keeping the Chartists out of the square, then not long completed, in 1848. After that, there had been intermittent bans on public assembly there. Recently the police had tried to break up all socialist rallies in public places – whether lawfully or not was a moot point.

The resurgence of protest there began on 8 February 1886 – Black Monday as it came to be called. Little trouble was expected that day. In the face of persistent unemployment, a Tory organisation called the Fair Trade League held a rally in the square to call for protectionism. A ragtag of unemployed who disagreed with the Fair Traders turned up, as well as an SDF counter-demonstration led by Hyndman, Burns and others. The overall numbers were more than expected – one estimate put it between 15,000 and 20,000. The few police did their best to keep the factions in different parts of the square. Burns, an effective stump orator but prone to get excited, allegedly told the crowd that hanging the House of Commons 'would be a waste of good rope ... The next time they met it would be better to go and sack the bakers' shops in the west of London. They had better die fighting than starving.' Some claimed he also said: 'Unless we get bread, they must get lead.'

Scuffles started (fig.2.7), and the police asked the SDF to lead their people off to Hyde Park, where demonstrations were usually allowed. This Burns proceeded to do, waving a red flag and marching via Pall Mall and St James's Street, with the roughs in the rear. Always happy to deliver another harangue, he halted provocatively in front of the Carlton Club, a Tory stronghold. At this point, some young bloods leaned out of the windows and mocked the marchers by throwing crusts of bread to them. It was the last straw. Club and shop windows were smashed all along St James's (fig.2.8), Piccadilly and right up to South Audley Street, as the unruly element made for the shops of Oxford Street. Burns led the vanguard to the Achilles statue in Hyde Park, where he urged them to show discipline and go home.

A middle-class panic ensued, and the Queen wrote to Gladstone in shock. The next day was foggy; there were rumours of riot and revolution. The authorities charged the SDF leaders with sedition and conspiracy, the Attorney General leading the prosecution. Only Burns had spoken like a sans-culotte, and even in his case there was confusion about just what he had said. The defendants were all acquitted, though the jury added the rider that their conduct had been 'inflammatory'. The verdict gave the SDF great heart. They now organised regular and peaceful demonstrations in Trafalgar Square, arguing for free speech in all

public places and for resolute government action to tackle joblessness. That prolonged the sense of nervousness palpable in London right through until the second set-piece, Bloody Sunday on 13 November 1887.

Trafalgar Square just then was a sadly appropriate place for demonstrations about unemployment. Every night between 200 to 400 destitute people slept there, 'huddled together on the seats, on the stones round the fountains and under the lions . . . the most terrible sight of open air human misery in Europe' (fig.2.8). Many chose the square because in the early hours they could slip off and try to get casual work shelling peas or sorting fruit in Covent Garden Market nearby. The local authority wanted the place cleared. In the summer of 1887, Sir Charles Warren, who had been put in as Commissioner of Police following the blunders of Black Monday, started to do so. But the unemployed came back; so too did the socialists and other sympathisers. In early November, Warren banned demonstrations in the square and made arrests when one was attempted.

Sunday the 13th became a trial of strength. In theory, the rally was organised by a body called the Metropolitan Radical Federation to protest against the imprisonment of some Irish MPs, notably William O'Brien, following the

2.7 Breaking up the Trafalgar Square demonstration on Black Monday, 8 February 1886. Most pictures of this kind are imaginative. (*Illustrated London News*, 13 February 1886)

2.8 Bread and soup being handed out during the small hours to the homeless in Trafalgar Square. (*Illustrated London News*, 18 October 1887)

passing of the latest Coercion Act in Ireland and the death of three men in the so-called Mitchelstown massacre. But that cause was soon forgotten in the general melee. The police were reinforced by the army (fig.2.9). They created a cordon round the square with strategic outposts, as the demonstrators were marching from three gathering points. A contingent from Clerkenwell Green led by William Morris was blocked in St Martin's Lane. The Paddington march got as far as the Haymarket, while the South Londoners under Burns and the Radical MP Cunninghame Graham were aggressively stopped at Westminster Bridge. But small groups including Burns and Graham did manage to sneak up to the Charing Cross edge of the square. Here more violence took place and the Riot Act was read. Two demonstrators died later from their injuries, but the martyr remembered from November 1887 came a week later. That was a young man called Alfred Linnell, a participant in an 'indignation' rally held on the following Sunday, which yet again tried to get into the square. He was trampled by a police horse, finally dying from his injuries some days afterwards. Linnell's funeral

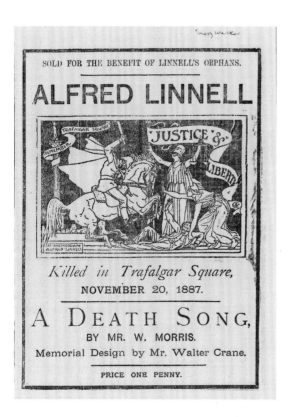

ALFRED LINNELL

JUSTICE & LIBERTY

Killed in Trafalgar Square,
NOVEMBER 20, 1887.

A DEATH SONG,
BY MR. W. MORRIS.
Memorial Design by Mr. Walter Crane.

PRICE ONE PENNY.

2.10 (above) Cover of death song for Alfred Linnell, trampled to death, 20 November 1887. Words by William Morris, design by Walter Crane. (Cheltenham Art Gallery and Museum, Emery Walker Library)

2.9 (left) Police hold back demonstrators from the centre of Trafalgar Square on Bloody Sunday, 13 November 1887, while Life Guards arrive. The demonstrators may not have got as close to Nelson's Column as the drawing suggests. (*Illustrated London News*, 19 November 1887)

cortege was preceded by a shield reading 'Killed in Trafalgar Square'. William Morris wrote a poem for the occasion, set to music by Malcolm Lawson and illustrated by Walter Crane (fig.2.10).

This time Burns was charged only with disorderly conduct, along with Graham; both got six weeks in Pentonville Prison. It did Burns no harm, setting him firmly on the national stage for his doughty defence of the cause. He came out the best-known working man in London. He was again to the fore in the successful dock strike of 1889, which along with the match girls' strike of 1888 symbolised the broadening of the trade union movement from skilled to unskilled labour. When the London County Council (LCC) was set up in 1889, Burns was elected for Battersea with a thumping majority and became the LCC's most esteemed working-class representative. He then quarrelled with Hyndman and the SDF, setting up a local caucus of his own. Burns went on to become an MP and eventually a 'Lib-Lab' minister in the Campbell-Bannerman and Asquith governments of 1905 onwards, when he sorely disappointed his old socialist comrades.

* * *

It is time to leave militant socialism and street politics, return to those poor sleepers in Trafalgar Square and see what was being said and done about them.

Slums, poverty, unemployment, disease and early death were endemic to London. There had always been protests against them, campaigns to combat them and charities to alleviate them. Concerted efforts to address the unique problems caused by the explosion in size of the world's biggest city go back at least to the 1830s – to the sanitary reforms of Edwin Chadwick, the heart-wringing writings of Dickens and much else. But fifty years later there came a definite turning point in consciousness, and a change and intensification in the actions taken to tackle the ongoing disaster that those Londoners who chose not to avert their eyes had constantly before them.

Why then? The incipient socialist movement was just a small contributory factor. More to the point were a serious slump in the economy and a series of bad winters. These affected the whole working class, but most of all they hit the vast numbers who earned their livelihood irregularly and casually, to use the word of the time, in the docks and markets, on building sites, as scavengers, street sellers, crossing sweepers and so forth. 'Outcast London', as it has been termed, was the intractable element of the urban population, disorganised, shiftless and elusive, the despair of those who tried to house, help and feed them. No one knew how many they were. Henry Mayhew, writing in the 1850s, estimated that about half the London workforce was casual; that had probably not much changed thirty years later. It must often have seemed in the 1880s as if half a century of effort to remedy the misery of urban life had been in vain. Slums could be cleared but renewed themselves elsewhere; mortality rates had hardly yet dropped.

HOW THE POOR LIVE

By GEORGE R. SIMS

With Sixty Illustrations by FREDERICK BARNARD

London
CHATTO & WINDUS, PICCADILLY·

2.11 Cover picture by Frederick Barnard for George R. Sims's *How the Poor Live*, 1883.

The starting signal for a fresh push towards action is often taken to be *The Bitter Cry of Outcast London*, a polemic published in 1883 by Andrew Mearns of the London Congregational Union. In fact, Mearns's book was symptom as much as cause. It emanated from a campaign of evangelism; the author's point of departure was to ask how and where his fellow Congregationalists should focus their mission efforts. At the time, the Churches of every denomination still looked upon the response to urban social problems as belonging primarily to them. But *The Bitter Cry* undermined a merely religious or moral response to deprivation in London by arguing that the main tenor of immediate action should be material not spiritual. By their charitable activities and public pronouncements many churchmen and churchwomen had long been expressing the same view. *The Bitter Cry* repeated all that with renewed emphasis, graphic examples and an urgent emotionality. Some of its sensational success derived from its title.

In part, *The Bitter Cry* was second-hand. Much of Mearns's material came from investigative articles by George R. Sims, republished in 1883 as a book called *How the Poor Live*. Sims was a zestful, jobbing playwright and journalist who never took himself that seriously, believing, to use a phrase of his, in life for life's sake. His style tended to be sentimental and 'cockney'; later generations have never quite forgiven him for his poem 'Christmas Day in the Workhouse'. Yet Sims was a lifelong Radical with a deep affection for Londoners of all classes. *How the Poor Live* (fig.2.11) came about after he was introduced to the Mint, a notorious slum area of Southwark, by a School Board inspector, Arthur B. Moss, and the headmistress of the Orange Street Board School, Elizabeth Burgwin. He went on to help Burgwin set up the most effective of several schemes to provide underfed schoolchildren with a meal each day. In 1889, Sims wrote a sequel to his investigations, *Horrible London*. Later, he edited two absorbing and delightfully illustrated volumes called *Living London*, published in 1902.

The new note in Sims' and Mearns's writing had much to do with shifts in the nature of Victorian journalism. The main pioneer was the *Pall Mall Gazette*. The *Pall Mall* had been founded in 1865 as the thinking reader's evening paper. After a change of ownership in 1880, its glittering cast of contributors and reviewers continued under the new editor, John Morley. Then Morley went into Parliament, to be succeeded by his deputy, the self-righteous W.T. Stead. Stead pulled off a series of brilliant coups, including a highly indiscreet interview with General 'Chinese' Gordon, already famous for his role in the defeat of the Taiping Rebellion. The resulting brou-ha-ha forced Gladstone's hand into sending Gordon off to Khartoum – with disastrous results.

Stead's most notorious stunt were his articles of July 1885, 'The Maiden Tribute of Modern Babylon'. With the connivance of Bramwell Booth of the Salvation Army, he bought a thirteen-year-old girl from her mother in Marylebone and took her to a brothel, in order to prove the reality of juvenile prostitution and the so-called white slave traffic – which even, it was alleged, included the supplying of young girls to King Leopold of the Belgians. Direct-action journalism of this kind was new. The ensuing hullabaloo succeeded in Stead's aim of forcing Parliament to pass the Criminal Law Amendment Bill that same year, which had been dilly-dallying for years in committees, and raised the age of consent from thirteen (it had been twelve till very recently) to sixteen. Stead, however, was prosecuted for abduction and sent down for three months, glorying in his martyrdom (fig.2.12). 'Never had I a pleasanter holiday, a more charming season of repose,' he said about Holloway Gaol, where he enjoyed privileged treatment. It all went to his head, and in the end may have cost him his editorship. The rest of Stead's quixotic career was something of a spiral; he got caught up in spiritualism and ended up one of the victims on the *Titanic*.

The reception of *The Bitter Cry*, Stead's editorship of the *Pall Mall* and his 'Maiden Tribute' articles all convey the climate of anxiety and sensation

2.12 W.T. Stead in convict uniform at Coldbath Fields Prison, November 1885. (Estelle W. Stead, *My Father: Personal and Spiritual Reminiscences*, 1913)

prevalent in London during the 1880s. One example of that is the Jack the Ripper saga, which has been a sordid obsession ever since the notorious Whitechapel killings in 1888 made the entirety of London shake in its shoes; miles from the scene, snug in his West Kensington bed, the five-year-old Compton Mackenzie was oppressed by 'nightly fears and fantasies'. These unsolved serial murders got so much attention partly because the East End, with its dark and intractable problems, was freshly in the national consciousness. They were reported in lurid terms and illustrations in a penny-dreadful paper called the *Illustrated Police News* (fig.2.13). The jittery mood of the time whetted the public appetite for reading about criminality, real or imaginary. So when *A Study in Scarlet* appeared in *Beeton's Christmas Annual* for 1887, Arthur Conan Doyle found a ready and ravenous appetite for his immortal detective, Sherlock Holmes (fig.2.14).

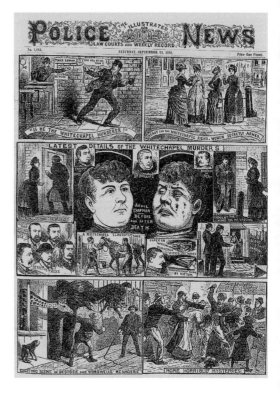

2.13 Sensational coverage of the Whitechapel murders. (*Illustrated Police News*, 22 September 1888)

For literate Londoners, the East End just then took on the guise of a new discovery, another dark continent that needed taming. The belief that it had been ignored hitherto is presented with some exaggeration by Walter Besant in his novel of 1882, *All Sorts and Conditions of Men*:

> Two millions of people, or thereabouts, live in the East End of London. That seems a good-sized population for an utterly unknown town. They have no institutions of their own to speak of, no public buildings of any importance, no municipality, no gentry, no carriages, no soldiers, no picture-galleries, no theatres, no opera – they have nothing. It is the fashion to believe that they are all paupers, which is a foolish and mischievous belief . . . Nobody goes east, no one wants to see the place; no one is curious about the way of life in the east . . . If anything happens in the east, people at the other end have to stop and think before they can remember where the place may be.

Besant goes on to offer a concrete suggestion about what might be done to cheer and enliven the East End; this was acted upon, as will be seen later in the chapter. His is the first and most optimistic of a notable clutch of novels about East London

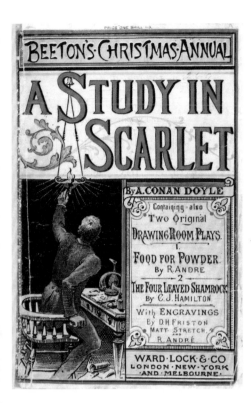

2.14 Cover of *Beeton's Christmas Annual*, 1887, featuring *A Study in Scarlet*, the first of Arthur Conan Doyle's Sherlock Holmes stories.

that thrust the area and its predicament before a wider public. Over their range, up to the mid-1890s, a darkening of diagnosis can be caught, as immigrants poured into the East End and its condition seemed to worsen. Commentators seldom pointed out that for most of its inhabitants, everyday life in a place like Whitechapel was not unendurably bad (fig.2.15).

A novel of quite another style, by the fastidious Henry James, likewise picks up the troubled tone of the time. *The Princess Casamassima*, published in 1886, is James's one attempt to penetrate the underside of London life. Its vignettes of charitable aristocrats visiting the poor, and of futile working-class conspirators dreaming in pubs, convey a moment close to despair:

They [the revolutionists] came oftener, this second winter, for the season was terribly hard; and as in that lower world one walked with one's ear nearer the ground, the deep perpetual groan of London misery seemed to swell and swell and form the whole undertone of life. The filthy air came into the place in the damp coats of silent men, and hung there till it brewed to a nauseous warmth, and ugly, serious faces squared themselves through it, and strong-smelling pipes contributed their element in a fierce, dogged manner which appeared to say that it now had to stand for everything – for bread and meat and beer, for shoes and blankets and the poor things at the pawnbroker's and the smokeless chimney at home.

Mearns, Stead and many others pricked consciences. Words can only move minds when the time is right, and *The Bitter Cry* touched a nerve. After it appeared, Lord Salisbury, leader of the Conservatives, wrote a long article on the housing conditions of the poor, setting off a fresh political debate. In 1884 Salisbury proposed a Royal Commission on the Housing of the Working Classes, which Gladstone's government, with support from the Queen, accepted. Because of the royal interest, the Prince of Wales was among the members. Hyndman and Morris were cynical about the initiative, calling it 'a favourite middle-class device for shirking responsibility and doing nothing'. They were right in the short term. The Commission heard mountains of evidence, but the final report and the resulting

Housing Act of 1885 were disappointments, adding to working-class frustration. Yet the findings did slowly percolate into policy, prompted as some believe by fresh stirrings of conscience following the Jack the Ripper murders. The stronger Housing Act of 1890, passed the year after the London County Council came into existence, was to mark the true start for municipal housing.

* * *

What meanwhile had the Churches been up to? Divided and competitive though they were, they had already done much in bringing piecemeal relief to the worst districts of London, learning from experience and mistakes. In the Church of England, there had been a slow withdrawal from the old belief, dating back to the years after Waterloo, that building churches was the best instrument for urban amelioration. The consequence had been to break London parishes up into ever-smaller units. Ambitious churches were built, gratifying the middle classes, but they had little impact on the rates of church attendance among the 'respectable' working classes, let alone the abject poor. In 1886, a Nonconformist magazine, the *British Weekly*, organised and published an informal census of church attendances in London. The first such exercise for 35 years, it was a rough pointer to whether church-building had made a difference. It had not.

Churches and chapels were certainly still being built in large numbers. Anglicans who put a premium on worship were forced to offer something fresh – livelier services, perhaps, greater congregational involvement, or richer architecture. St Cuthbert's, Philbeach Gardens, Earl's Court, for instance, of 1884–7, emerged out of the old system of parish subdivision. Its charismatic vicar, Henry Westall, peddled an Anglo-Catholic ritualism that drew a congregation from far beyond his tiny parish. Westall divided his flock up into guilds to enrich the bare Gothic fabric of his church with their own hands, carving ornament,

making vestments and so forth; here participation was the key. Another High Church foundation, Holy Redeemer, Clerkenwell, of 1887–8, was a mission church in a poor district but with establishment backing (Gladstone laid the foundation stone) and nuns to assist the clergy. Here the sensation was J.D. Sedding's Catholic-looking architecture, half-Italian and half in Wren's City-church idiom (fig.2.16). The aesthete Walter Pater was impressed.

But in deprived areas missions, halls, clubs and refuges had by now become the main thrust of go-ahead activity for all the denominations. 'In 1880 the air of England was thick with … "hostels", "settlements", "halls" and "missions", to enable the rich to understand and sympathise with the poor', recalled one commentator.

A good example is the parish of St Giles-in-the-Fields at the edge of the West End. For ages this had contained some of London's grimmest districts. Road projects had eliminated some slums, only for the poorest to crowd into other bad districts like Seven Dials and the courts off Drury Lane. All the competing Churches in St Giles were trying to raise their game above mere preaching or token visiting by charitable ladies. The Baptists, for instance, had lost their core of respectable adherents from their old-established chapel as tradespeople decamped to the suburbs, so they turned it into the St Giles Christian Mission. Here food and refuge for the dregs of society were the priority, seconded where possible by conversion; a famous supper was held every year for discharged prisoners. At the time, the Methodists were drawing their scattered efforts together into the West London Mission, founded by Hugh Price Hughes in 1887; St Giles became a focus of this work, and in due course housed the Mission's headquarters. Some other initiatives were less strictly denominational. These included the first London medical mission, set up in Endell Street by a Crimea veteran and 'healer-preacher', George Saunders. By 1890 the slum streets and alleys of St Giles were riddled with clubs, missions and refuges, all doing their small bit in the face of overwhelming deprivation.

Not everyone who plunged into work of this kind knew just what they were trying to achieve. In the semi-fictional *Mark Rutherford's Deliverance* (1885), William Hale White portrays M'Kay, a restless spirit who has been brought up upon the Bible, cannot believe it anymore, but has 'a passionate desire to reform the world'. He takes a room in a street off Drury Lane, which he proposes to keep open 'as a place to which those who wished might resort at different times, and find some quietude, instruction, and what fortifying thoughts he could collect to enable men to endure their almost unendurable sufferings. He did not intend to teach theology … He meant to teach Christ in the proper sense of the word.' M'Kay and Rutherford keep it up for a couple of years and manage to help one or two individuals before they learn 'that we could not make the slightest impression on Drury Lane proper'.

The faith-fuelled Christians kept on at things. Slowly, missionary work was becoming better co-ordinated. But it had yet to supplant the zeal of individuals who threw themselves into the fray and could grow lonely, ill, lose their faith or even wear themselves to death in the process. An example from St Giles was David Rice-Jones, appointed in 1883 by the Anglicans' London Diocesan Home Mission to the Drury Lane area, then rife with criminality, prostitution and rough-sleeping. Rice-Jones, with help from his wife, set up a mission and refuge for boys in a run-down house near Lincoln's Inn Fields, wrote articles published in 1884 as *In the Slums*, opened a second refuge behind the Drury Lane Theatre, and dreamed of starting a settlement. Then suddenly he transferred to a country parish. There his wife died. Soon afterwards he was taken into an asylum and died too; his children emigrated to Canada.

Earlier, the liberal intellectual J.R. Green had suffered similar setbacks. Green had laboured hard in East End parishes during the 1860s, then lost his faith and health and withdrew into writing history. Green's death in 1883 was the spark for Mrs Humphry Ward's *Robert Elsmere* (1888), one of the publishing sensations of the

2.17 Mrs Humphry Ward. Photograph by Francis Barraud, *c.*1888. (Wellcome Collection)

decade. Gladstone read the book when it came out and was gripped by it, pronouncing it as unputdownable as Thucydides.

Elsmere is a brilliant young Oxford graduate who gets ordained, marries and takes a country parish. But he is 'perverted' by the rationalist squire, loses his belief in miracles and resigns out of conscience. He comes up to London, plunges into social work in the East End and founds the New Brotherhood of Christ, which promotes the pre-eminent example of Jesus's life and teachings but denies his godhead. Uncertain what to do with Elsmere at the end, the author gives him consumption, sends him (like Marx) to Algiers and kills him off. His settlement work continues, we are led to believe. And indeed Mrs Humphry Ward (fig.2.17) went on to found a settlement herself in 1890 – what is now Mary Ward House in Bloomsbury.

Robert Elsmere struck a chord because educated young people of both sexes with a conscience were often on the horns of something like its hero's dilemma at this time. Darwin's ideas had percolated deep enough to ruffle simpler Christian beliefs. The settlement movement was one way out. The usual idea was that alumni from the public schools and universities should live for a spell in some poor part of London, giving what help they could. The Oxford liberal theologians and dons of the day had produced a crop of serious young men who felt they ought to serve, at home or in the Empire. If some were sure about the Church, others were not. All types could find a settlement to suit them.

The cream of the liberals went to Toynbee Hall, a settlement that had begun as an extension of work started by Samuel Barnett in his Whitechapel parish during the 1870s. Barnett had begun his East End ministry with orthodox attitudes: 'the principle of our work is that we aim at decreasing, not suffering but SIN', he pronounced in 1877. Gradually that changed. What Whitechapel most needed, Barnett came to believe, was social and cultural enlightenment. So he started an art exhibition and brought down young men from Oxford to help. Then came *The Bitter Cry*. In November 1883 Barnett gave a speech at a meeting in Oxford called 'Settlements of University Men in Great Towns', describing the plight of lone clergy in poor London parishes like his and calling for graduates to come to their aid.

Toynbee Hall, called after the young Oxford don Arnold Toynbee, who had been one of Barnett's helpers in Whitechapel but died that year, gave a secular slant to the settlement movement. Religion took a back seat. When it started off in 1884–5, the

tone was not missionary – more like a piece of Oxbridge plonked down in the East End, with university extension lectures, art shows (fig.2.18), Shakespeare societies and so forth bolted on. Among the early residents was the budding architect and artworker C.R. Ashbee, who prettified the dining room with sunflowers and college crests. Toynbee Hall was as much about educating these young men (fig.2.19) by getting them to understand working-class lives as about bettering the material lot of the East Enders. The settlement-movement ideal was to bring the classes and skills together, not in order to eliminate class differences but so that workers and gentlefolk could develop a wiser form of interdependence through what has been called the 'gift relationship'. The better-off often got the most benefit. In the Edwardian years, after William Beveridge and others arrived, Toynbee became a kind of research centre into urban poverty and unemployment.

Hyndman's magazine *Justice* was predictably cynical about Toynbee Hall. 'It seems to us', it wrote, 'that if the East End of London could and would return the compliment and send a colony of the workers to the Universities to teach the gilded youths on the Isis and the Cam how to do a little useful work and how to live on something less than £300 a year, that would be a much better arrangement.' Church leaders too were wary, because Toynbee downgraded

2.18 'Art in Whitechapel – loan exhibition of pictures in St Jude's School House, Commercial Street, E.' (*The Graphic*, 22 November 1884)

2.19 Toynbee Hall, the first cohort, with Henrietta and Samuel Barnett in the centre. The half-comic, languishing attitudes bespeak an Oxbridge college group of the day.

mission and salvation. Before it could even get going, to the annoyance of Barnett and his thrusting wife Henrietta, a second group of Oxford men had founded Oxford House, Bethnal Green, which was explicitly religious in its aims (fig.2.20).

These were the most famous of the 1880s university settlements. Yet well beforehand, Toynbee Hall and Oxford House had been beaten to it by other initiatives, often emanating from the public schools. At first most were externally supported missions rather than full settlements. Eton chose Hackney Wick, while Harrow opted for a barren zone between Notting Hill, North Kensington and Shepherd's Bush 'amid the laundries and piggeries and brick-kilns of the extreme West'; both raised ambitious churches to mark their endeavours. Marlborough College supported a mission church in outlying Tottenham, while Tonbridge took on a parish near King's Cross where the school owned property and was profiting from the rents. The first women's university settlement was founded in 1889 off the Blackfriars Road in Southwark, drawing in supporters from all the Oxbridge women's colleges and concentrating on education and local clubs; Mayfield House in Bethnal Green, sponsored by the Cheltenham Ladies' College, followed on a little later. The movement became strategically organised, as colleges asked advice from bishops and others about where they should 'plant'. Oxford tended to take the East End, while Cambridge was pointed by Bishop Thorold of Rochester towards South London, at that time in his diocese.

During the 1880s, the settlement movement was mostly Anglican-based, with Nonconformists and non-sectarians picking up on it a little later. Meanwhile, movements of other kinds were already busy. Foremost was the Salvation Army,

which grew out of East End work in the 1860s but only took its name in 1878 and inaugurated its famous musical tradition in the '80s. Its founder General Booth's manifesto *In Darkest England, and the Way Out* came out in 1890, largely ghost-written for him by Stead (fig.2.21). Working-class or lower middle-class to the core, the 'Sally Army' promoted combativeness. In fighting vice, drink and sin, it demanded total commitment from its soldiers. It soon put middle-class backs up and also generated an opposing 'skeleton army' of ruffians who baited the Salvationists at every turn. The scuffles and fights between the two were relished by both sides in the early years. Not that the Salvation Army was unconstructive. Its male and bonneted female troops ventured into dens of iniquity and hovels of sickness where others feared to tread; it started its own efficient series of hostels after 1888; and it was among the organisations to promote farm settlements and emigration of slum children to Canada and Australia. By this time, however, the 'white colonies' were becoming less inclined to absorb the refuse of London's population, as they had been doing since Lord Shaftesbury and his supporters started such schemes back in the 1840s.

* * *

From General Booth to Charles Booth (fig.2.22), hailed in his lifetime as the 'founder of the science of cities'. A wealthy Tory businessman with statistical

2.20 Oxford House, Bethnal Green. The High Church response to Toynbee Hall, started in 1884. These are the permanent buildings, of 1890–2.

2.21 Frontispiece to *In Darkest England, and the Way Out*, published by General Booth for the Salvation Army in 1890. The chromolithographic image stresses the Army's anti-urban dispersal and pro-emigration policies. The title refers to H.M. Stanley's *In Darkest Africa*, published only months before.

skills and a social conscience, Booth was stimulated by *The Bitter Cry* but piqued by its lack of objective data, and he loathed Stead's sensationalism. He began his investigations by talking to the Barnetts, the housing reformer and manager Octavia Hill and others. If someone would look carefully at the census returns for 1881, he believed, the true facts about the poor would become known. So when Hyndman and the SDF claimed in 1885 that 25 per cent of London's population lived in extreme poverty, and the *Pall Mall Gazette* echoed the claim, Booth decided to refute them. Off his own bat, he set up a 'Board of Statistical Research' and began his enquiry, relying on a few doughty helpers – Beatrice Potter, later Beatrice Webb, is the most famous. They started with Tower Hamlets, talking to clergy and employers, collecting data from School Board visitors, investigating the lives of half a million people and jotting down facts in small notebooks. This mammoth exercise took little more than a year, 1886–7. No less astonishing was the result. Booth concluded that in Tower Hamlets up to 35 per cent, not 25 per cent, were living 'at all times more or less in want'. Hyndman had been right after all, so it seemed. From these first findings, the sociological concept of the poverty line originated. Recently, the accuracy of Booth's researches has been disputed and his poverty line condemned as 'arbitrary'. What no one disputes is that they shook and galvanised his contemporaries.

2.22 Charles Booth, 'founder of the science of cities'. (Wellcome Collection)

Booth and his helpers did not isolate poverty. To get at its causes they looked into the conditions of work in Tower Hamlets and the whole social face of the East End. Joblessness apart, the labour issue then under most scrutiny was sweating – in other words the employment of underpaid workers, especially women, on piecework for long hours in cramped premises, often their own homes, and under the sway of demanding middlemen in place of the old-style master craftsmen. Sweating was an old, London-wide problem with many causes, but it was getting worse in the 1880s. If the East End clothing, footwear and furniture trades were the main focus of concern, the casualisation of dock labour following the collapse of trade in the upriver docks was little different. In the clothing industry, the spread of the personal sewing machine stimulated the growing mass market for cheap clothes. All this put new demands on workers' productivity; standards and wages fell together. John Burnett, a trade unionist turned civil servant, undertook a first official analysis of East End sweating in 1887, but Booth's survey examined the issues with a better grasp of the local context. The House of Lords appointed a Select Committee in 1888.

In Whitechapel and Stepney there was an extra factor: Jewish immigration. Since Tsar Alexander II's assassination in 1881 and the onset of reprisals, poor Russian and Polish Jews had been leaving in growing numbers. Just how many settled in East London is disputed, but the arrivals were certainly in their many thousands; at the start of the influx, Russians and Poles, nearly all Jews, made up 55 per cent of immigrants into Whitechapel. Booth estimated the East End Jewish population at about 40,000, by no means all recent immigrants, of whom 15,000 were 'quite poor', another 15,000 moderately so, and 10,000 reasonably comfortable. Many of the arrivals went into the clothing or the boot and shoe trades, since these skills were in demand. Motivated and diligent, they undercut their rivals and often produced better-quality goods.

One of the several remarkable East End novels of the time, Israel Zangwill's *Children of the Ghetto* (1892) celebrated this influx:

> Into the heart of East London there poured from Russia, from Poland, from Germany, from Holland, streams of Jewish exiles, refugees, settlers . . . all rich in their cheerfulness, their industry and their cleverness. The majority bore with them nothing but their phylacteries and praying shawls, and a good-natured contempt for Christians and Christianity. For the Jew has rarely been embittered by persecution.

Opposition came from several sources: from established Jews, who felt their community was being dragged down by the impoverished and (as Zangwill hinted) sometimes truculent newcomers; from trade unionists, especially in the boot and shoe trade, who feared the undercutting of existing workers; and from a swelling chorus of commentators and politicians.

The earliest full articulation of the anti-Jewish-immigrant case came from a radical journalist and eugenicist, Arnold White, in his book of 1886, *The Problems of a Great City*. White claimed to be philo-Semitic, but through his Society for the Suppression of the Immigration of Destitute Aliens he became increasingly the reverse. As more poor Jews arrived without legal impediment, the overall tone of criticism and anxiety became shriller and more persistent, to be stilled only in 1905 when the Aliens Act sharply restricted numbers. Not everyone was hostile to the East End Jews. Beatrice Potter, for instance, examining the tailoring trade on Booth's behalf, thought they had exerted a good moral influence: 'As a citizen of our many-sided metropolis [the Jew] is unmoved by those gusts of passion which lead to drunkenness and crime.'

After Tower Hamlets, Booth moved on, tackling first Shoreditch, Hackney and Bethnal Green and after that the rest of London, in a massive set of volumes and maps that come in three series: poverty, industry and religious influences (fig.2.23). They are a priceless resource for understanding the late-Victorian metropolis.

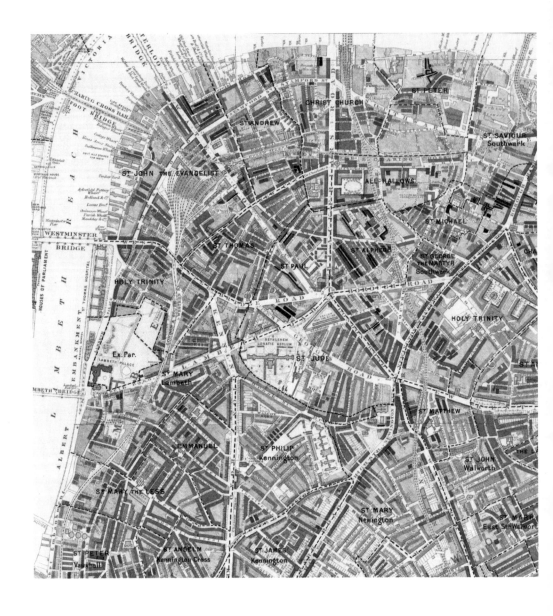

The first volume, published in 1889, was praised as 'the one practical outcome of all the gush that had recently been poured out'. Now everyone really knew, or believed they knew, how things stood. And where Booth stood, remarkably for a Tory businessman, was that some sort of limited socialism was necessary. The State, he believed, must take responsibility for the 'helpless and hopeless'. Charity and the Churches were not enough.

2.23 Sheet 9 of Booth's *Descriptive Map of London Poverty*, 1898–9, showing parts of Lambeth and Southwark, divided by parish and with the famous colouring system showing degrees of poverty from dark (worst) to light (best).

* * *

2.24 Pear Tree Court,
Clerkenwell Close.
Peabody block dwellings
of 1883–4.

2.25 Gladstone Avenue,
Noel Park. Rowland
Plumbe, architect, for the
Artizans', Labourers',
and General Dwellings
Company, 1883 onwards.

2.26 Red Cross Cottages,
Southwark. Elijah Hoole,
architect, for Octavia Hill,
1887–8.

Here we stand on the threshold of the 1890s. In 1889 the London County Council takes over from the Metropolitan Board of Works and becomes a directly elected government for London, albeit with limited powers. The Board of Works comes to grief, ostensibly for some trivial corruption issues, in reality because of the accumulating pressures and agitations of the 1880s. Soon the LCC is building housing. The vestries too do their bit with new baths, laundries, libraries, dispensaries and mortuaries to stand alongside the ramifying network of board schools. Meanwhile, an array of hospitals and institutions is springing up around London's fringes to refine the old systems of the Poor Law and mitigate their harshness.

Social conditions in the metropolis may have been little better in 1890 than 1880. But they were different by 1900, in great measure because of the outcry and efforts of the 1880s. Most municipal institutions and services available by then could not have been imagined twenty years before. When Hyndman set up his Federation, when the settlement movement began, and when the Royal Commission of 1884–5 sifted the record of the 'Five Per Cent Philanthropy' companies and their barrack-like blocks of 'model housing', that any broad range of social provision for Londoners might be administered by a local arm of the state was hardly foreseen. The School Board's work excepted, the many reforms undertaken were bitty and particular, struggling with one pocket or other of poverty, criminality, disease or slum. What emerged from the 1880s was a growing consciousness that the problems were so great in scale that they had to be tackled systematically; no existing agency was up the task. That is why Charles Booth's statistical investigations mattered.

Take the housing question. Most reformers agreed that the philanthropic blocks of flats that had become the standard solution for housing the artisan classes in London (fig.2.24) were just a depressing palliative: 'millions of tons of brute brick and mortar,' George Gissing the novelist called them in 1889, 'crushing the spirit as you gaze'. Dispersal was now in the air. Farm colonies, not inner-city workhouses, might be the answer for paupers, Samuel Barnett and General Booth agreed. As for the self-sufficient, would it not be better to get them out of the centre into decent small houses or maisonette-flats in the suburbs, where land costs were lower and there was space and air? But that shifted the working classes miles from their employment, and few could afford to pay the cost of travel.

There had already been ineffective attempts to force the railway companies to run subsidised trains. The first legislation to have teeth was the Cheap Trains Act of 1883, but that too took a long time to yield results, as the example of the Noel Park Estate at Wood Green, started just then, reveals. Noel Park (fig.2.25) was the next major venture of the Artizans', Labourers', and General Dwellings Company after its Shaftesbury Park and Queen's Park estates. Built from Rowland Plumbe's designs, it was marketed as a 'Suburban Workman's Colony', accessible via subsidised morning and evening trains. Yet it proved unaffordable to most working families, because the railway companies would not co-operate. Though lobbying them achieved some concessions, Noel Park was soon in trouble, with much of it still unlet in 1887. The big growth in cheap trains only came in the next decade.

One of the great reform figures of the age was Octavia Hill. She had been drawn into the housing business in the 1860s as a protégée of Ruskin's, managing a small block of slum property just by making sure that the place was kept clean, the rent was paid on time, and tenants were treated with a brisk humanity. Her common-sense approach paid off. By the 1880s Hill had a big portfolio of old properties, which she or her affiliates looked after with success. She was resolutely against the looming blocks of the philanthropic companies – indeed she was against all made-to-measure working-class housing, as she robustly told the Royal Commission. Then something changed. The Ecclesiastical Commissioners asked Hill to look after some of their Southwark and Camberwell properties that had been badly managed. Here from the late 1880s she did start to build, beginning with the delightful Red Cross Cottages (fig.2.26) and going on to larger developments. She stuck to her dislike of blocks and of municipal enterprise, and always believed houses should be pretty and small-scale. But she was also mutedly starting to recognise, as had others before her, that London's housing could not be left to enlightened conservativism, mission and charitable activity.

* * *

Technical education – an unappealing name but another burning topic of the day – demonstrates the same inching towards co-ordination. As the century wore on, Britain seemed to be falling behind its industrial competitors, Germany above all, for want of skilled workers. By the 1880s the School Board for London was building bigger and better-equipped elementary schools. Yet higher up the scale, there was no system of secondary education, just a ragbag of fee-paying schools. Nor, as industry and commerce specialised, could artisans or clerks avail themselves of anything better than piecemeal training to replace the moribund apprenticeship system.

The glimmer of an answer came from reform in a different sphere. The City of London had been sitting on large sums of money locked up in charities created centuries before for the benefit of residents in its tiny parishes – well over a hundred in all. But the population of the City had plummeted, from some 131,000 in 1851 to 50,000 in 1881, and was still dropping. The notorious case was St Mildred, Bread Street, which had about £800 per annum to spend on a population of 46, 'of whom but four or five slept in the parish and none was poor'. Over a quarter of this income was spent on junketing: 'Breakfast and dinner on Ascension-day, audit dinner and refreshment after vestries and visiting parish estates and cab hire.' Other City parishes were hardly better; only four had any population to speak of. Might not these endowed charities, ecclesiastical and secular, be released for the benefit of London as a whole?

The cause was taken up by an alliance of dedicated reformers, among whom James Bryce, Ulsterman, academic, jurist and MP, merits pride of place. Despicably, the time-servers of the City Corporation and their cronies in Parliament fought the change tooth and nail. By dint of perseverance and compromise, Bryce pushed through the City of London Parochial Charities Act in 1883. That was half the battle won. The ball now passed to the Charity Commission, a body set up some years before to reorganise English charities. The Commission had first to list and value the manifold City parish charities, and then devise a workable scheme for spending the money. All the while, City interests sought to divert or delay the process, so that the independent City Parochial Foundation could only be established in 1891.

Meanwhile there was some leeway for interim distribution; this the Charity Commissioners cautiously went about. Some of the money helped to save commons and open spaces around London, which earlier preservation campaigns had been too poorly resourced to do. More went towards education, a domain familiar to the Commissioners since the 1860s, when they had reorganised the charities that funded the nation's public and grammar schools. Technical training was a logical next step, but on what model?

Tentatively, the Commission plumped for the polytechnic. By this was meant not the elite colleges of that name pioneered in France and Germany, but friendly places that would combine social and training facilities for working-class men – and women. The name came about accidentally. Quintin Hogg was a sugar and tea merchant who had vowed to spend all his spare time and money on charity. He began by running a Christian youth club, to which he then added evening classes offering technical training. So successful was the combination that when the old Royal Polytechnic Institution in Regent Street, part science museum and part popular spectacle, failed in 1881, Hogg took it over. He kept the name and recast it as 'The Polytechnic', mixing secondary, evening and trades classes (fig.2.27) with opportunities for recreation and a smattering of religion. From an initial 2,000, his roll shot up to 6,800 after the first winter.

One of the Charity Commissioners went to see Hogg's Polytechnic in 1887, was impressed, and recommended it as the model to support. Soon assorted businessmen got together to create similar polytechnics in industrial districts of South London at Woolwich, Deptford, Elephant and Castle, and Battersea (fig.2.28). All four were in formation by 1890, once again mixing recreation with training. They became the basis of today's University of Greenwich, Goldsmiths College, South Bank University and University of Surrey. Like the Regent Street original, the London polytechnics mostly began life as precarious institutions in adapted premises, supported by private donations and meagre doles from the Charity Commission. Stability came only in the 1890s, after extra funding was supplied by the newly created City Parochial Foundation and the LCC. In this way, voluntary initiatives were gradually drawn into a genuine system. An assortment of technical colleges – monotechnics, they were sometimes called – followed on

2.27 Typing class at The Polytechnic, Regent Street, c.1902. (University of Westminster Archives)

2.28 Battersea
Polytechnic, Battersea
Park Road, c.1900. E.W.
Mountford, architect.
This was the only early
polytechnic to have
entirely purpose-designed
buildings. (University of
Surrey Archives)

to provide training for specific trades. The recreational element tended to drop
away over time, though Regent Street fiercely maintained it for years.

Hogg was not alone in championing a balance between training and recreation.
Walter Besant had called for something of the kind in *All Sorts and Conditions of
Men*, which proposed that the East End could be simultaneously educated and
cheered up by means of a 'Palace of Delight' to be built in Stepney. In the novel,
the palace is preposterously built by a philanthropic millionairess posing as an
East End dressmaker. But far from leaving things to fiction, Besant to his credit
pressed on and sought funds for his idea. Only after the Charity Commissioners
supported it could his dream be built, assisted by conscience-money from City
companies. The project was delayed by over-grand designs commissioned from
E.R. Robson, the School Board's architect. Finally, the People's Palace, as it was
called, arose in Mile End (fig.2.29). In a moment of triumph, Queen Victoria
came to open it in 1887. Here too, after a shaky start, 'delight' took second place
behind prosaic educational goals. It is now the core of Queen Mary University
of London.

* * *

Now for something completely different: two great technical changes that began
to revolutionise London life in the 1880s.

'We have had our house at Kensington fitted up with the telephone, and this

2.29 The People's Palace,
Mile End. E.R. Robson's
final scheme. (*Illustrated
London News*, 8 June 1891)

little instrument causes a complete reform in our housekeeping arrangements,'
wrote 'A Lady' in about 1885. The spread of the instrument was dramatic.
Alexander Graham Bell lectured in London in 1877 and demonstrated his
invention to the Queen the next year, when the first British company offered
its services. The earliest exchange was opened at Coleman Street in the City in
August 1879. Soon afterwards, two rivals amalgamated as the United Telephone
Company, which dominated the London business for the next twenty years. The
Post Office already ran telegraphy, but kept out of commercial telephony till the
turn of the century. The telegraph was efficient and much valued. But though
good enough, say, for foreign stock-market prices, it could not offer an instant
exchange of views.

Predictably, most early subscribers for phones were business people – lawyers,
bankers, stockbrokers and journalists who needed information urgently. At first
all calls were local; many companies just had an internal system between office
floors or between different London premises. But the instrument spread like
wildfire, allowing the Kensington lady to plan her routine, and phone as far as
Brighton (fig.2.30). All calls were put through by an operator at the exchange,
and this rapidly became thought of as women's employment. By 1888, there were
about 4,800 lines in London, dealt with by 23 exchanges. That was too many,

2.30 The early telephone. Top left, a reporter phones in copy from Parliament to *The Times*. Bottom left, United Telephone Company's headquarters in Coleman Street, City of London. Centre, women working the exchanges. Right top and bottom, a man and a woman phone between London and Brighton. (*The Graphic*, 1 September 1883)

and in the 1890s rationalisation took place. Even so, London continued to lag far behind the major American cities in its uptake of the telephone.

Like the telegraph, the phone requires electricity. The parallel revolution of the decade was the spread of electric lighting. The first such lighting, which came in at the end of the 1870s, consisted of arc lights, in which the current leapt across a gap between two carbon rods. Arc light was powerful but harsh in quality and noisy – there was a continuous hiss or crackle. So apart from a few novelty installations in shops and theatres, the various rival arc-light systems were confined to locations such as streets, factories, docks and yards. Paris tried it out in its streets first, mainly in the guise of the so-called Jablochkoff candle. In London, street-lighting experiments started with a section of Victoria Embankment, lit by the Jablochkoff system in December 1878, and extended to Waterloo Bridge the following autumn. In 1881 the City Corporation tested three different arc-light systems, Brush, Jablochkoff and Siemens, near the Mansion House (fig.2.31). Further trials followed. But after the incandescent light came in – in other words the vacuum bulb with filament, widely available from 1881 – the scope of arc lights retracted. Incandescent light was weak to start with, so that its first public outings for street lighting along Holborn Viaduct and Newgate Street failed to impress. Where it scored was inside buildings, not least houses (fig.2.32). It didn't smell or ruin fabrics and pictures, as did gas. It also had a delicacy and an ornamental quality, so those who could afford it installed the low-wattage bulbs in pretty tiers and bunches.

The new lights would have spread far faster if Joseph Chamberlain, then President of the Board of Trade, hadn't messed things up with the Electric Lighting Act of 1882, which imposed a very restrictive regime. Companies had little incentive to invest in plant, because they were not allowed to dig up public streets, while the districts that each was allowed to supply were drawn very small and the length of the concessions was unattractively short. So most of the earliest installations were for private concerns like the Grosvenor Gallery, which installed plant in 1884 to light its own building, going on to supply shops nearby in Bond Street and elsewhere via overhead cable. The restrictions were slightly eased by a second Act in 1888. By then, the brilliant young Sebastian de Ferranti was managing the Grosvenor Gallery operation, extending its reach and dreaming of a London-wide electricity supply from a single massive source of power. His Deptford Power Station, the model for future electricity supply systems, opened late in 1889. But it was far less successful than he hoped. Legislative restrictions still held it back, and Ferranti soon left to go into manufacturing electrical equipment. Meanwhile the gas companies fought back fiercely, maintaining their grip on London's street lighting far into the twentieth century. Gas consumption was growing fast in the 1880s, while in

2.31 Siemens arc lights at Mansion House, 1881. (J.D. Scott, *Siemens Brothers 1858–1958*, 1958)

2.32 Drawing room, from Robert Hammond, *The Electric Light in Our Homes*, 1884. The wall sconces are equipped with circular brass reflectors. (Science & Society Picture Library 10421347)

the next decade the Welsbach gas mantle proved an effective indoor competitor to the electric light bulb.

* * *

One of the early electrical suppliers was R.E.B. Crompton, who started his Kensington Court Electric Light Company to service the development of that name in 1886, and built a house for himself behind its generating station. Kensington Court had been started in 1882 by Jonathan Carr, fresh from his triumph at Bedford Park. Its houses were designed by another smart architect, J.J. Stevenson (fig.2.33), and it had the most go-ahead technical features yet of any London housing scheme: subways for service pipes and wires along the streets, and hydraulic lifts in the houses instead of back stairs. Behind the development was a dedicated accumulator station for the hydraulic power alongside the stabling, which was squashed into a multi-level court at the back with ramps so as to keep the smelly horse world clear of the houses. Electricity was probably foreseen from the start.

But Kensington Court was never completed. Less than half of it got built before Carr failed. A property company proceeded to buy the rest of the land and cover it with so-called 'mansion flats'. The change is symbolic. During the 1880s, the demand for up-and-down middle-class terrace houses dwindles, spelling the beginning of the end for this archetypal London building-type. Smaller suburban terraces carry on in countless numbers up to the First World War, often only two storeys in height, with ugly extensions barging out at the back to compensate for the abolition of damp, dark basements. But the grander terrace house is on its last legs by 1900, except in a few prime locations. The formal London square collapses with it. Among the last is Nevern Square, Earl's Court, which starts around 1880 and maunders on for years, filling up with retired army officers. Around its edges the big blocks of flats start to rise.

It was Jonathan Carr's own venture in this new line, the grandiose Whitehall Court looming over Victoria Embankment (fig.2.34), that landed Kensington Court in trouble, gobbling up his capital and forcing him to sell up. Carr was not canny enough to weather the tricky financial climate of the 1880s. After his failure, the finance and construction of Whitehall Court passed on to underlings of a more notorious speculator, Jabez Balfour, Mayor of Croydon, MP, and the brains behind the Liberator Building Society. The moral was that blocks of mansion flats needed much higher levels of capitalisation than terrace houses, which could be built a few at a time. When flats began to go up in large numbers from the 1880s, they seem always to have been snapped up fast, suggesting that there was no English aversion to the type, as is often supposed. Their take-up coincides with increasing sophistication and flexibility in the money market for housing. That did not prevent the Liberator from crashing

2.33 Kensington Court. Perspective of houses designed by J.J. Stevenson. (*Building News,* 7 May 1886)

91

in 1892, bringing ruin to a multitude of small investors and a prison sentence for Balfour.

Most of the new blocks of flats rose to only five or six storeys (fig.2.35). There were a few monsters, usually built in phases: Queen Anne's Mansions, the first, started as early as 1873; Albert Hall Mansions; Whitehall Court and so on. Some of these bigger blocks toyed at first with including communal dining rooms to service the flats, so they were not much different from hotels, but the idea didn't catch on. All such flats of course had lifts, hydraulic to start with. A related type was the purpose-built block of flats over shops, often at corners (fig.2.37). These might be residential chambers in the West End; or accommodation for shopkeepers, their staff, or anyone willing to live on a main road and over a shop. Middle-class flat life on the level was tighter, cosier and more urban than in the old up-and-down house. Perhaps it suited childless people the best (figs 2.37, 2.38).

On the topic of height in London buildings, there is a might-have-been question. Why didn't London go high in the 1880s, as Chicago and New York did? It had the hydraulic lift, it had the iron frame (rapidly becoming the steel

2.34 Whitehall Court from Victoria Embankment Gardens. Archer and Green, architects, 1885–90. (Chris Redgrave)

2.35 Flats of about 1890 in Warwick Road, Earl's Court.

frame), so it was all feasible. Rents were also higher in central London during late Victorian times than in the great American cities, as they generally remain today. The same big building-types, notably speculative offices and warehouses, were going up at the same time on both sides of the Atlantic. Yet the leap was never made.

The simplest explanation is that the regulatory climate in London was much more cautious. For reasons going back to 1666, the authorities were terrified by fire. Although there were some disastrous Victorian blazes, London could be proud of its modern fire record. In formulating and enforcing rules about construction the Metropolitan Fire Brigade tended to have the last say, and under Captain Shaw, the celebrated martinet who commanded it all through the 1870s and '80s, it was ultra-conservative. The brigade was good at checking on things like proper fire exits in theatres and party walls. But it showed scant interest in new technology (even its dashing helmets were out of date), and its ladders were not high or extensible enough to cope with heights above 80 ft; nor was water pressure for the hoses reliable above that height. So there was an implicit limit of 80 ft to the cornice, although that was not explicitly laid down till 1894. In these circumstances most architects and clients seem to have quietly gone along with the rules. This caution seems not to have damaged London businesses very much.

It has never been convincingly shown that building high, even in commercial centres, is rational or necessary. Whatever the reasons that London refused the American hunger for height in the 1880s, in view of later experience we can be glad that the challenge was declined.

2.36 Flats over shops at 1–5 Mount Street, Mayfair, 1889. Ernest George and Peto, architects. (Historic England Archive, BL09521)

* * *

This chapter may have given the impression that Londoners had no fun in the 1880s. Choosing from countless examples to the contrary, here is a coda on exhibitions.

For London, though not for Paris, Chicago and other of the world's major cities, the officially sponsored prestigious international exhibition was over after 1862. Smaller shows took place at South Kensington in 1871–4, to be followed in the '80s by a specialised series on fisheries, health and inventions – all dull and worthy sequels to the 1851 original. A Colonial and Indian Exhibition in 1886, the first to be confined to Britain and its dominions, proved more popular. It seems to have sparked the ambitious idea of the Imperial Institute, planned to hold some

2.37, 2.38 Bourgeois flat life. Left, Mrs Thomson in her sitting room, Macclesfield Chambers, Shaftesbury Avenue, 1898. (Historic England Archive, BB75/05754). Right, G.K. Chesterton in his flat at Overstrand Mansions, Battersea Park, 1904. (From *The Tatler*)

sort of permanent exhibition. The project turned out ill-fated. Thomas Huxley pronounced it 'already a failure' before it was begun; it finally opened in 1893 to very limited enthusiasm.

Private promoters now seized their chance. Two simultaneous schemes sprang up, both on the margins of Kensington and close to a railway. Olympia, opened in 1886 next to Addison Road Station, was a conventional large exhibition hall of a kind familiar by then, notably from the Royal Agricultural Hall in Islington. The formula was to erect a large station-type shed and hire it to anyone who would take it for sporting tournaments, trade shows or even theatricals. The results were inevitably uneven.

Livelier and odder was the Earl's Court Exhibition. The sponsors were an American consortium of businessmen marshalled by an Englishman, J.R. Whitley. They bought some land tortuously squeezed between railway tracks, with access from three separate stations – Earl's Court, West Brompton and West Kensington. It began in 1887 with just a long, narrow and flimsy building for trade displays, flanked by circus-type attractions: a switchback, toboggan slide and bandstand to one side, and then across some railway lines an arena with half a grandstand (fig.2.39). It all looked precarious.

The first year's exhibition naturally had an American theme. Whitley pulled off the coup of enlisting Colonel William Cody's 'Buffalo Bill Roughriders and

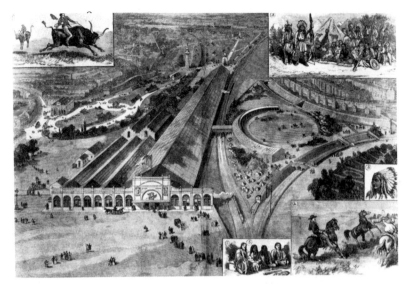

2.39 Bird's-eye view
of the Earl's Court
Exhibition as laid out for
the American Exhibition,
1887. Exhibition halls to
the left of the railway,
arena to the right.
(*Illustrated London News*,
16 April 1887)

Redskin Show', which he ran into by chance on a business trip to Washington. This, the famous troupe's debut abroad, introduced Britain to the cult of the Wild West. For five months, Cody's cowboys whooped it up in the arena, thrilling the crowds, supported by hapless Sioux warriors and their squaws (fig.2.40). Gladstone came, the Prince and Princess of Wales came, finally the Queen too came and witnessed a shortened version of the show. She was, according to *The Times*, more interested in 'the Indian babies or papooses. Two of these were presented . . . and she was pleased to shake their hands and pat their painted cheeks.' The Earl's Court Exhibition was saved. It went on to acquire Britain's first Ferris wheel.

There was a sequel that November at the Royal Agricultural Hall. Two of the rough riders, Broncho Charley and Marve Beardsley, were persuaded to take part in a six-day competitive test between horses and bicycles. Some said this was to compare their merits for postal purposes, but for the teeming spectators it was just for thrills. According to the *Illustrated Police News*, the rough riders won, 'covering in the 48 hours (eight hours a day) 814 miles 4 laps, while the champion cyclists were about two miles behind. The horsemen employed thirty horses, and gained much by the agility with which they changed their horses.' But the poor cyclists were pedalling on primitive machines with solid tyres. Once Dunlop's pneumatic tyres came in after 1889, bicycles would carry all before them. The contest must have been a relief after the events of Bloody Sunday a few days previously.

2.40 Vignettes of 'Buffalo Bill's Wild West' encampment at the American Exhibition, Earl's Court, 1887. (*The Graphic*, 7 May 1887)

3

London in the 1890s

Here is a famous poem with a Latin title, 'Non sum qualis eram bonae sub regno Cynarae'.

LAST night, ah, yesternight, betwixt her lips and mine
There fell thy shadow, Cynara! thy breath was shed
Upon my soul between the kisses and the wine;
And I was desolate and sick of an old passion,
Yea, I was desolate and bowed my head:
I have been faithful to thee, Cynara! in my fashion.

All night upon mine heart I felt her warm heart beat,
Night-long within mine arms in love and sleep she lay;
Surely the kisses of her bought red mouth were sweet;
But I was desolate and sick of an old passion,
When I awoke and found the dawn was gray:
I have been faithful to thee, Cynara! in my fashion.

I have forgot much, Cynara! gone with the wind,
Flung roses, roses riotously with the throng,
Dancing, to put thy pale, lost lilies out of mind;
But I was desolate and sick of an old passion,
Yea, all the time, because the dance was long:
I have been faithful to thee, Cynara! in my fashion.

I cried for madder music and for stronger wine,
But when the feast is finished and the lamps expire,
Then falls thy shadow, Cynara! the night is thine;
And I am desolate and sick of an old passion,
Yea, hungry for the lips of my desire:
I have been faithful to thee, Cynara! in my fashion.

3.2 (right) Ernest
Dowson as a young man
at Oxford, 1886. No later
picture makes him look
more cheerful. (*The Poems
of Ernest Dowson*, 1905)

3.1 (far right) The Cock
Tavern, Shaftesbury
Avenue. The pub where
'Non sum qualis eram'
was written. (*Building
News*, 28 October 1887)

Nothing could be more remote in mood and tone from London in the 1890s, you might think. Yet this, the finest English lyric poem of the decade, was written in the Cock Tavern, Shaftesbury Avenue (fig.3.1), on 6 February 1891. There its 23-year-old author, Ernest Dowson (fig.3.2), would start his evening's drinking, before joining other young bohemians round the corner at the Crown, Charing Cross Road. Often he got completely drunk and had to stay the night with one of his boon companions. In the morning, Dowson would pull himself together none too early and drag his way out to Limehouse.

Here, beside a down-at-heel Thames wharf, lay the solitary office of the Dry Dock Corporation, a small family firm started by Dowson's grandfather that prepared ocean-going boats for their voyages. By 1890 it was on the verge of collapse. The big ships had long been moving downriver, first to the Royal Docks and then to faraway Tilbury miles east, leaving upriver wharves (Fig. 3.3) precarious. The great London dock strike of 1889 had ended in victory of sorts for the men, but for the owners it meant extra pressure.

Ernest's father Alfred Dowson, like Ernest himself, was a weak, tubercular man with aesthetic tastes and little interest in the business. Needing the money, the family made a feeble effort to make the dock work. But the father was seldom there, and Ernest seems to have spent much of the day at his literary endeavours

before sloping off to the West End. Occasionally, friends visited Dowson in Limehouse. One was Frank Harris, who remembered:

> We dined in a frowsy room behind a bar on a bare table without a napkin: the food was almost uneatable, the drink poisonous. Afterwards Dowson took me round to places of amusement! The memory of it all – a nightmare! I can still hear a girl droning out an interminable song meant to be lively and gay; still see a woman clog-dancing just to show glimpses of old, thin legs, smiling grotesquely the while with a toothless mouth; still remember Dowson hopelessly drunk at the end screaming with rage and vomiting insults – a wretched experience.

Worse was to come. In 1894, Dowson's father died in his new flat at Albert Mansions, Battersea Park, from an overdose of chloral hydrate, possibly on purpose; six months later his mother hanged herself. Ernest got rid of the dock at last and moved to France, drifting there for most of the rest of his short life. The year before he had written: 'though I hate London more than the pains of Hell, I am kept here for a personal reason and must try to keep here, although

3.4 Clubbing artists of the 1890s. Left to right, D.S. MacColl, C.W. Furse, Max Beerbohm, Wilson Steer and Walter Sickert, painted by William Rothenstein, 1894. (Bridgeman Images)

almost any other place would suit me better.' He had a few successes, for instance a playlet called *The Pierrot of the Minute*, illustrated with reluctance by Aubrey Beardsley, who found Dowson grubby. He worked quite hard, but never again reached the heights of 'Non sum qualis eram'. Like many literary people, he despised London but needed it. In the end he crawled back, to die in abject want at a friend's house in Catford, aged 32, in February 1900.

Dowson was well equipped technically as a poet. The title of his great lyric comes from Horace, and its subject matter may be impersonal. Still, he seems to have known a good deal about the bought red mouths of prostitutes. There was certainly a real-life Cynara: Adelaide Foltinowicz, 'Missie' to the poet, the daughter of a Polish café owner in Sherwood Street, Piccadilly, where he liked to eat and show off a bit. Like everything in his life that turned out grim too. Missie was twelve or thirteen when Dowson met her, fourteen or fifteen when the famous poem came out. She was the 'personal reason' that kept him in town; hers were the 'pale, lost lilies' he tried to forget about. Eventually Missie got bored and married a tailor; Dowson was distraught.

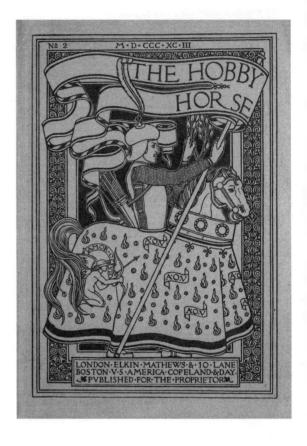

3.5 *The Hobby Horse*, cover of the second series, designed by Herbert Horne, 1893. Produced by Elkin Mathews and John Lane, founders of the Bodley Head and publishers of *The Yellow Book*. (William Morris Gallery)

Ernest Dowson can stand for a certain quality of London artistic life in the 1890s: its risk-taking, its excess, its fragility, its aestheticism, its will to fail and therefore its failure. The usual name for this is decadence, a term borrowed from French culture. France, or rather Paris, became fashionable again in the London of the 1890s to a degree it hadn't been for some time. The French decadent writers – Baudelaire, Flaubert, Huysmans, Maupassant, Verlaine and so on – enjoyed a popularity (and in Verlaine's case a welcome) which their earlier counterparts had not had, as did the Symbolist painters – Puvis de Chavannes, Gustave Moreau and the seedy Félicien Rops. Compton Mackenzie recalled being introduced to the decadents at the age of sixteen, starting with Théophile Gautier's *Mademoiselle de Maupin*. 'Much of the fascination of symbolism was that one never really grasped what the poet was writing about,' he remembered; 'in some way this confirmed one's belief in its wonderful interpretation of existence.'

Also from France came the penchant for the artistic clique, and for the nurturing of a self-conscious metropolitan elite or avant-garde. Elite and avant-garde are terms derived from French military terminology. They came into cultural circles via the Saint-Simonian movement earlier in the century, which put flesh on the bones of Shelley's conceit that poets (not, by the way, artists) are 'the unacknowledged legislators of the world'. Naturally, there had always been cliques and coteries in London cultural life – around Samuel Johnson and around Dickens, for instance, clubs for artists, and movements like Pre-Raphaelitism. But the belief in an autonomous world of artists and writers with its own morality and rights strengthened in the London of the 1890s. Some of it had to do with the changing nature of patronage. An artist like Whistler, painting what he wanted to paint and flinging it in the public's face, as Ruskin claimed, called the shots in a way that Wilkie or even Turner never could.

These cliques or sets overlapped. Dowson belonged marginally to the circle of the Rhymers' Club, which often met in the Old Cheshire Cheese off Fleet Street. Its central figures were W.B. Yeats and his companions of the time: Lionel Johnson, who died not long after Dowson, falling drunk off a bar stool, and Arthur Symons, who published a mediocre volume of verse called *London Nights* in 1895. But Dowson was also in touch with the circle around Oscar Wilde, whose favoured outlets were *The Yellow Book* and later *The Savoy*. Then there was the Chelsea art set (fig.3.4), featuring painters who sought to mimic Whistler's style of being an artist as much as his style of art: Charles Conder, Walter Sickert, Wilson Steer, D.S. MacColl, William Rothenstein and the reclusive Charles Ricketts and Charles Shannon, with bigger guns like Sargent on the edge. Not all of them were in London together. There was much flitting around, to France especially. But they all needed London for the galleries, the theatres and the plethoric magazines of the day.

Just two such cliques put the applied arts high on their agenda. One, seldom remembered today, was identified by a place rather than a precise set: Whiteladies, otherwise known as the Fitzroy Settlement. This was a Georgian house in Fitzroy Street which the architect and designer A.H. Mackmurdo turned into a short-lived centre for his Century Guild circle in the late 1880s and early 1890s, long before anyone had heard of Fitzrovia. *The Century Guild Hobby Horse* (1884–94) was a forerunner of the art magazines that proliferated in the 1890s (fig.3.5). At Fitzroy Street there were cartoons by Selwyn Image all the way up the stairs, blinds on the windows by day as well as by night, and white-painted woodwork throughout.

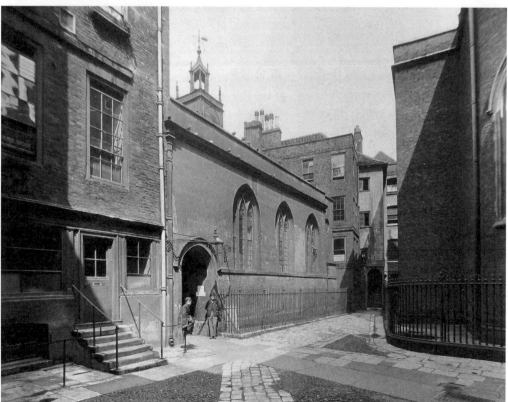

Herbert Horne had rooms here for a time, as did Lionel Johnson, who seldom got up before lunch. Among sundry gatherings at Whiteladies was a memorable Rhymers' Club event of 1891 when Oscar Wilde, at the peak of his charisma, stole the show from Yeats and Walter Crane. The house disappeared in the Second World War.

The second such clique turned out to be more enduring. That was the Art Workers' Guild, founded by Norman Shaw's leading assistants in 1884 as a talking shop for young architects. Influenced by the political and cultural trends of the day, the Guild extended into a pressure group for reforming the applied arts, dominated though never monopolised by the admirers of William Morris and Philip Webb. Between 1888 and 1894 it met in Barnard's Inn, Holborn, today the venue of the Gresham Society lectures (fig.3.6); and between 1894 and 1914 in Clifford's Inn, Chancery Lane (fig.3.7), alas destroyed. These quaint old-world halls, relics from redundant Inns of Chancery, betrayed the backward-lookingness embedded in Art Workers' Guild psychology. Something of that dogged traditionalism lived on after the Guild finally moved to the hallowed premises it has occupied since 1914 in Queen Square.

Oscar Wilde (fig.3.8) is the nonpareil symbol of decadent culture. It is fashionable today to underline the Irishness of Wilde, as of Yeats, Bernard Shaw and George Moore. But in their years of early glory and infamy, they were all Londoners first and foremost. The halcyon years for Wilde were 1889 to 1895, when, in his biographer Richard Ellmann's words, 'aestheticism was revised and perfected' as a form of higher ethics based on individual freedom, a kind of 'narcissistic socialism' allowing the exploration of hitherto forbidden areas of thought and behaviour. For Ellmann and many others, the 1890s come to a close with the Wilde trial. The rest is a slide towards imperialism, the Diamond Jubilee, and the Boer War.

Matthew Arnold told the young Wilde that 'one must shake off London life before one can do one's best work'. But if Wilde wrote much of that best work away from metropolitan distractions and allurements, it was mostly set in London. His brief run of triumphs, after not a few theatrical flops, began in 1890 with The Picture of Dorian Gray. Today this novelette reads like a vehicle for Wilde's best witticisms and reversals of conventional morality; it is never as convincingly macabre as the best of Poe or Stevenson or even Conan Doyle. All the scenes take place in the standard smart London settings of the day: a bachelor flat in Albany; a club in St James's; a grand house in Grosvenor Square; a low-life music hall; an opium den. There are even some sallies about the tedium of philanthropy in the East End, whither Dorian Gray and an aunt of Lord Henry Wotton, his Svengali

3.6 The hall at Barnard's Inn, Holborn, in 1892, when used by the Art Workers' Guild. Some mementoes still owned by the Guild today are visible. (Collage 356630)

3.7 Clifford's Inn, exterior of hall, Chancery Lane, probably in 1903. Home of the Art Workers' Guild, 1894–1914. Demolished in 1934.

3.8 The arrest of Oscar Wilde at the Cadogan Hotel. (Peter Jackson Collection/Look and Learn: *Illustrated Police Budget*, 13 April 1895)

figure, go to entertain the poor. On this Wilde is mock-severe, quipping that philanthropy is sentimentality, when science is what is needed: 'It is the problem of slavery, and we try to solve it by amusing the slaves.'

The settings for the real-life episodes in Wilde's crowded years of triumph and tragedy are worth remark. *Lady Windermere's Fan*, the first of the four famous comedies, was staged in 1892 at the St James's Theatre, long since gone but in those days a haunt of the West End elite. *A Woman of No Importance* followed at the Haymarket in 1893; *An Ideal Husband* again at the Haymarket in January

3.9 One of the
illustrations by Aubrey
Beardsley for *Le Morte
Darthur*, c.1892–3.

HOW LA BEALE
ISOVD WROTE TO
SIR TRISTRAM

1895; and *The Importance of Being Earnest* back at St James's just one month after. During these years Wilde was living a reckless life away from his wife back in Chelsea, drinking hot port at the Crown with Dowson and other cronies after performances, dodging between modern hotels such as the Albemarle, the Berkeley and the Savoy, sometimes with Lord Alfred Douglas, sometimes on his own, bedding messenger boys and so on. Clearly he was out of control. It was at the Albemarle Club that Douglas's father, the Marquess of Queensberry, left his notorious illiterate note, 'For Oscar Wilde posing somdomite', which led to the disastrous libel suit and then the criminal trial; while the arrest took place on 6 April 1895 at another recently opened hotel, the Cadogan (fig.3.8), a scene evoked by Betjeman in one of his best poems. That was the end of Wilde's London life, if his brief sojourns in Pentonville and Wandsworth Prisons are excepted, and a terrible moment when, as he was being transferred to Reading Gaol, he was identified and spat at while standing on the platform at Clapham Junction in the rain.

The reaction over the collapse of morality and religion after the Wilde trial engulfed many careers. It nearly even put paid to Lord Rosebery, Liberal Prime Minister from 1894 to not long after the date of Wilde's arrest. Queensberry's oldest boy, Lord Drumlanrig, who had died mysteriously a few months before, had been close to Rosebery. A suspicion that homosexuality lay at the bottom of that relationship, it's often claimed, was what made Queensberry so angry and vengeful about his second son's involvement with Wilde.

The artist who suffered most in the reaction was Aubrey Beardsley, naughty and outrageous, decadent and obsessed by sex, but neither evidently homosexual nor close to Wilde. Beardsley stands head and shoulders over others in the London magazine- and book-design world of the 1890s. Yet he was only briefly a man about town. He started out as an office clerk, shifting with his mother and sister from one Pimlico lodging to the next until they could afford a house; but for the last two years of his pathetically short life – he died in 1898 aged only 25 – he was largely abroad trying to stem his consumption.

Beardsley's first big break came in 1892 when he was recommended to the publisher J.M. Dent to illustrate Malory's *Le Morte Darthur* (fig.3.9). The result was an implicit criticism of the beautiful but cumbrous Kelmscott editions of classic texts then being printed by William Morris. Beardsley revolutionised techniques of illustration with the help of the new zinc blocks, which accurately transferred his exquisite contrasts of fine line and matt-black plane through the process of photographic line-block printing. That remained a constant, as his styles evolved alongside his obsessive reading – illustrating texts was always the mainstay of his work. *Le Morte Darthur* had some risqué scenes, as did *Salome* and Beardsley's plates

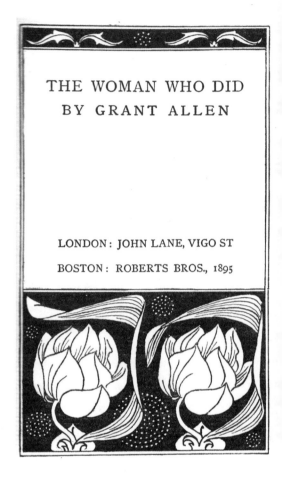

THE WOMAN WHO DID
BY GRANT ALLEN

LONDON : JOHN LANE, VIGO ST
BOSTON : ROBERTS BROS., 1895

3.10 Title-page to Grant Allen's novel, *The Woman Who Did*, with vignettes by Aubrey Beardsley, 1895.

and covers for *The Yellow Book*, so he became *persona non grata* to the publishing establishment after the reaction of 1895. He was kept going by Leonard Smithers, a pornographer of stalwart character, who started *The Savoy* in 1896 as a rival to the bowdlerised *Yellow Book*. Smithers also paid Beardsley to illustrate much else, notoriously Aristophanes' *Lysistrata*. Like some other leading lights of the 1890s, Beardsley became a Catholic convert at the end and wanted Smithers to destroy the *Lysistrata* drawings. Besides the sensational stuff, there is also much excellent Beardsley book work, for instance a simple title-page for Grant Allen's *The Woman Who Did* (fig.3.10), a very '90s novel about a middle-class woman who decides to have a baby but not get married, with the usual consequences.

* * *

There was room for other styles of writers and poems besides the decadents. Here is a poem written by an author who tore through London like an express train in the early 1890s and out the other side again. The title is again Latin, 'In Partibus', short for 'in the land of the infidels'.

The 'buses run to Battersea,
The 'buses run to Bow
The 'buses run to Westbourne Grove
And Nottinghill also;
But I am sick of London town
From Shepherd's Bush to Bow.

I see the smut upon my cuff
And feel him on my nose;
I cannot leave my window wide
When gentle zephyr blows,
Because he brings disgusting things
And drops 'em on my "clo'es".

The sky, a greasy soup-toureen,
Shuts down atop my brow.
Yes, I have sighed for London town
And I have got it now:
And half of it is fog and filth,
And half is fog and row.

And when I take my nightly prowl
'Tis passing good to meet
The pious Briton lugging home
His wife and daughter sweet,
Through four packed miles of seething vice
Thrust out upon the street.

Earth holds no horror like to this
In any land displayed,
From Suez unto Sandy Hook,
From Calais to Port Said;
And 'twas to hide their heathendom
The beastly fog was made.

I cannot tell when dawn is near,
Or when the day is done,
Because I always see the gas
And never see the sun,
And now, methinks, I do not care
A cuss for either one.

But stay, there was an orange, or
An aged egg its yolk;
It might have been a Pears' balloon
Or Barnum's latest joke:
I took it for the sun and wept
To watch it through the smoke.

It's Oh to see the morn ablaze
Above the mango-tope,
When homeward through the dewy cane
The little jackals lope,
And half Bengal heaves into view,
New-washed—with sunlight soap.

It's Oh for one deep whisky peg
When Christmas winds are blowing,
When all the men you ever knew,

And all you've ceased from knowing,
Are "entered for the Tournament,
And everything that's going."

But I consort with long-haired things
In velvet collar-rolls,
Who talk about the Aims of Art,
And "theories" and "goals,"
And moo and coo with women-folk
About their blessed souls.

But that they call "psychology"
Is lack of liver pill,
And all that blights their tender souls
Is eating till they're ill,
And their chief way of winning goals
Consists of sitting still.

It's Oh to meet an Army man,
Set up, and trimmed and taut,
Who does not spout hashed libraries
Or think the next man's thought
And walks as though he owned himself,
And hogs his bristles short.

Hear now, a voice across the seas
To kin beyond my ken,
If ye have ever filled an hour
With stories from my pen,
For pity's sake send some one here
To bring me news of men!

The 'buses run to Islington,
To Highgate and Soho,
To Hammersmith and Kew therewith
And Camberwell also,
But I can only murmur " 'Bus"
From Shepherd's Bush to Bow.

'In Partibus' speaks in the unmistakeable voice of Rudyard Kipling (fig.3.11). It is not a first-rate poem and Kipling omitted it from his collected works. But what a breath of air after all the preciousness of the decadents, and how much it says about the reaction that broke after the Wilde arrest!

Kipling arrived in London from India in 1889 at the age of 24 to further his career. Though an outsider, he had excellent connections; for instance, Burne-Jones was his uncle by marriage. He took rooms for a year over a sausage shop in Villiers Street beside Charing Cross Station, watching London's low life from his windows. His poem was written not for a British audience but for the *Civil and Military Gazette*, one of the Indian papers via which he had made his youthful reputation. Here is what he said about it in a letter:

3.11 Rudyard Kipling, drawn by William Strang, 1898. (National Portrait Gallery 2919)

> An evil-evil day. Rose up in the morn at 9 and found the gloom of the Pit upon the land, a yellow fog through which the engines at Charing Cross whistled agonizedly one to the other and I could see the switch-boxes lit up with cheap and yellow gas when the electric light was manifestly needed. These English are fools: which things so moved me to despair that I sat down and wrote a doleful ditty for nothing in particular which I later packed up for the C & M Gazette. It was called 'In Partibus' and was the wail of a fog-bound exile howling for Sunlight.

Kipling soon became well known in London, moving in a different milieu from the aesthetes and decadents. The magazines that published him were mostly the robust, pro-imperial ones run by men like W.E. Henley and Andrew Lang. Kipling was to become associated with his support for the Empire, which deepened after he met Cecil Rhodes in the mid-1890s. Yet despite his veneer of populism he too had his inward side. While in Villiers Street he wrote a curious first novel called *The Light that Failed*, about an illustrator-painter who goes blind – not the bookish, Beardsley-ite type, but a war artist who has seen action in the Sudan and returns there to commit virtual suicide when he can't paint any more. It is no masterpiece and its love side is kittenish, but it makes serious points about art. It also sketches in a virile version of the life in West End bachelor flats popular among bohemian circles during the 1890s.

The other point of convergence between Kipling and the decadents is the music hall. He never liked mainstream theatre, but he was fascinated by the 'halls' and often visited Gatti's under Charing Cross Station down the road from his chambers, picking up the idiom and the cockney slang, and also spying on the clientele, just as Sickert did (fig.3.13). These forays widened Kipling's poetic range

Balham   Royal Duchess-Theatre

3.12 The Royal Duchess Theatre, Balham, opened in 1899. W.G.R. Sprague, architect and manager.

and led to the two volumes of *Barrack-Room Ballads* (1892), his first big hit in the home country. Half-Indian, half-English and often military in subject matter, the poems are more poignant and artistic versions of music-hall songs. Indeed, they reached the music-hall audiences and were hardly out of print for the next fifty years.

Music hall reached its apogee in the 1890s. Most of the many new theatres built in London around this time (six in Shaftesbury Avenue alone) were glorified music halls or variety theatres, openly or under the skin. That was especially so in the suburbs, where a theatre-building boom took hold in the final years of the century, buoyed up by the lure of profits from popular entertainment. Its fruits included the Princess of Wales's Theatre, Kennington; the Royal Duchess Theatre, Balham (fig.3.12); the Alexandra, Stoke Newington; the Granville, Walham Green; and the Shakespeare, Lavender Hill. They were often large and pretentious; almost all have perished now, destroyed by bombs or the invasive cinema.

In central London too theatres were putting on scale and weight. They reached new proportions in Frank Matcham's Hippodrome of 1900 (fig.3.14), soon to be outdone by his even bigger Coliseum. Unsubsidised as they were, such costly theatres could not survive on highbrow fare alone. The Royal English Opera House at Cambridge Circus, designed by T.E. Collcutt, opened to grand éclat with Arthur Sullivan's *Ivanhoe* in 1891, but within a year had to be converted into a variety palace (fig.3.15). Sneaking up on the side meanwhile was the infant cinema. The Lumière brothers first exhibited at the Regent Street Polytechnic in 1896. As yet films seemed no threat to theatre and music hall. Compton Mackenzie later recalled: 'There was no premonition of what the Cinematoscope at the Empire or the Animatoscope at the Alhambra portended; they seemed just a kind of amusing conjuring trick.'

The decadents were as enthralled by music halls as Kipling. Much of Arthur Symons's *London Nights* is about the life of the halls; like many hangers-on, he got his girls from them – chorus girls, dancers, stars when possible. In *The Importance of Being Earnest*, there's a sly reference to one of the allurements of the halls, when Algernon says to Jack, 'Well, we might trot round to the Empire at ten?' The audience would have known just what that was about: picking up high-class tarts.

3.13 (above) The gallery at the Old Bedford Music Hall, Camden Town, by Walter Sickert, c.1895. (Walker Art Gallery, Liverpool)

3.14 (above right) The London Hippodrome in 1902. Frank Matcham, architect. To the right on the Charing Cross Road front, The Crown pub where Dowson and friends drank has been rebuilt. (Historic England Archive, BL17229)

3.15 (right) The Palace Theatre, Cambridge Circus, built as the Royal English Opera House to designs by T.E. Collcutt, 1890–1. (Wikimedia Commons, Matt May)

The 'attack' on the Empire, Leicester Square, was one of the London sensations in 1894. Today a cinema, the Empire had been built as a grand variety theatre ten years earlier. It was taken over by George Edwardes, the proprietor of the Gaiety Theatre and from 1893 the promoter of Daly's, a second variety theatre almost next door to the Empire. Edwardes was the cleverest of the variety proprietor-managers. He fed the public with a melange of ballets, musicals and tableaux put on with great extravagance and skill. Shows of this kind aren't taken seriously today, which may be our loss. As they were produced just before photographs started to be taken regularly inside theatres, we have only drawings to make sense of these sumptuous spectacles.

3.16 'Three Graces' from the Empire, Leicester Square.

Edwardes pushed the boat out, off stage and on. The on-stage phenomenon was the development of *poses plastiques* – static tableaux of scantily clad girls. This was an old Victorian game, often in fake representation of some classical theme (figs 3.16, 3.17) and involving the use of body stockings. At Cambridge Circus, the reincarnated Palace (after the Royal English Opera House failed) specialised in these *tableaux vivants*. But the Empire gave them wider currency and new twists such as scenes on the beach. As for the off-stage side of things, the Empire had a horseshoe promenade area just outside the stalls, where drinks were sold and the audience could move around and mingle during performances. Music hall or variety was all-round entertainment; what happened on stage was never all that mattered. Especially round ten o'clock, when the Empire was about to let out, the poshest and most gaudily dressed prostitutes of a prostitute-packed city would flock into the promenade to pick up their clients (fig.3.18). Something similar but more furtive went on at the back of the pit for homosexuals.

In 1894 Mrs Ormiston Chant decided to do something about the Empire. Laura Ormiston Chant was a committed feminist and suffragist with a finger in many pies. She had just attended something called the World's Parliament of Religions in Chicago. She was an editor of the National Vigilance Association's magazine and a campaigner for social purity, social vigilance and rational recreation – three puritan battle-cries of the time. She was no mere idealist, having been a sister at the London Hospital, where she saw what vice could do. Later she took nurses out to the front in the short Greco-Turkish War of 1897. In short, a brave and formidable woman.

3.17 (above left) Sketches of three chaste *tableaux vivants* from the Empire.

3.18 (above right) The promenade at the Empire. Later pictures of the same scene are more lurid. (Charles Eyre Pascoe, *London of To-Day*, 1894)

Some American friends of Mrs Chant went to the Empire one day to hear Albert Chevalier sing some 'coster' songs. The report they brought back caused her to alert the National Vigilance Association. She and her colleagues attended the Empire five times, taking detailed notes about the proceedings, on stage and off. Thus armed, they applied to the Theatres and Music Halls' Committee of the London County Council for the licence of the Empire not to be renewed. The campaign spread further afield. For instance, an ally of Mrs Chant's, Carina Reed, was tasked with investigating the nearby Oxford Music Hall. These ladies wished to reform the music halls, not close them, and to persuade them to put on musical entertainments with a higher tone on Sundays.

The press had a field day, mainly taking the side of Edwardes and the Empire, and the public responded in kind. Street pedlars even sold little balloons depicting the campaigner that they would inflate and collapse on their trays, calling: 'Mrs Ormiston Chant faints when she sees the Tabalo Veevongs at the Hempire. One penny.' There was much crass anti-feminist comment, but also a reasoned defence of a liberal and artistic theatre from some critics who were as anxious for the performers' welfare as Mrs Chant.

When it came to the crunch, the LCC adjudicated by a narrow margin that the Empire must reform itself, stop selling drinks on the promenade and break up the space. Yet despite this enforced clean-up, little real change seems to have happened. The promenade at the Empire was still in full swing up to the time that Arnold Bennett wrote his wartime bestseller *The Pretty Lady* (1918); in fact, it was the First World War that put a stop to it. Vice – or fun – will always find a way. And the LCC, which was only supposed to ensure that theatres were structurally safe, not to police what went on in them, seemed to be meddling in morality and went down a notch in public esteem.

* * *

The exuberant theatrical world was the tip of an iceberg. London in the 1890s was humming with entertainments of every kind and level. Never had leisure provision been so prolific or elaborate, in token of there being more disposable income across all classes of metropolitan society. To put it another way, 'Leisure activities could make the deprivations suffered by many in other aspects of their life more bearable'.

Pubs must come first (figs 3.19, 3.20). The 1890s was the golden age of the London pub, as Mark Girouard has eloquently explained. 'The pubs then were bigger and brighter, their lamps more enormous, their glass more elaborate, their fittings more sumptuous than they had ever been before or were to be again.' Not that there were more pubs than before; hundreds of small and scruffy ones were being shut down by freeholders or licensing magistrates. But their replacements, invariably 'tied houses' promoted by brewer-owners, were astonishing and astonish still: bumptious essays fizzing with finials, gables and ornament, ebullient inside and out, revelling in the potential of electric light to dazzle the darkest nooks and corners. These bounteous palaces offered relief and contrast to the drab and poky working man's home. That had once been the prerogative of churches. But in a church, awe and admiration were tempered by deference. In a pub the punter could relax amid extravagance.

3.19, 3.20 The Dover Castle Hotel, Westminster Bridge Road, Lambeth. Treadwell and Martin, architects, for the pub developer Charles Best, 1894–5. Exterior, and looking through bar towards dining room. The Dover Castle started as a high-class establishment with dining and accommodation. Today it is a food store. (Historic England Archive, BL13501, 13522)

3.21 Interior of the Flying Horse (formerly the Tottenham), Oxford Street. Saville and Martin, architects, 1892–3 (Chris Redgrave)

One can pick out only a handful of surviving interiors: the Prince Alfred, Maida Vale; The Flying Horse, Oxford Street (fig.3.21); two Salisburys, one in St Martin's Lane, the other in suburban Harringay; the Queens, Crouch End; the Assembly House, Kentish Town; the Boston Arms, Tufnell Park; the Boleyn Tavern, Upton Park; the Falcon, Clapham Junction; and the Princess Louise, Holborn. All have been mauled or tinkered with – small bars united and snob screens removed – yet all retain a glorious relish in primness and restraint abandoned.

The great boom in pub-building started in 1896 under a solidly established Tory government, always supportive of the brewing trade (hence the two Salisburys), and carried on with mounting frenzy for three years. Huge sums were paid for pubs by breweries and speculators: £52,000 in 1892 for a pub that had cost £7,000 eight years before; later, £80,000 for the Royal Oak, Bayswater; £86,000 for the Crown, Cricklewood Broadway; and the top price of £98,000 for the Victoria, King's Cross. 'The smash came in 1899,' reports Girouard. 'Almost

3.22 The Circus
Restaurant, Oxford
Street, interior in 1886.
A small, good-class
restaurant run by
Augusto Gianella from
the canton of Ticino,
Switzerland. (Historic
England Archive,
BL06366)

all of the pubs put up for sale at the beginning of that year failed to reach their
reserve and were bought in.' Spectacular bankruptcies ensued, and for the first
years of the new century few pubs were built. 'From 1900 the public house was
looking for a new image but, in London, at any rate, it took some time to find it.'

In parallel with the pubs went an explosion of restaurants and cafeterias – or
tea shops, as the latter were usually known. The old-style Dickensian chop house
with boxes for an all-male clientele, mostly located in the City, had long been
withering away. 'In the days of my early youth,' recalled the journalist Edmund
Yates, 'there was, I suppose, scarcely a capital city in Europe so badly provided
with eating houses as ours; not numerically, for there were plenty of them, but the
quality was all round bad.' The earliest chic restaurants tended to be associated
with hotels or theatres, but by 1890 there were plenty of independent ones in
the West End, following in the wake of Frederick Gordon's Holborn Restaurant,
which could seat 2,000 and was much patronised for club and corporate dinners.
Many were managed by foreigners, with French or Swiss-Italian chefs (fig. 3.23).

Lower down the scale, chains of refreshment rooms had been proliferating
since the 1860s. The pioneers were Spiers and Pond, who started off at railway
stations and exhibitions. Lockhart's Cocoa Rooms, part of a spurt in temperance
hostelries dating from the 1870s, reached London from Liverpool in 1879 and
flourished in poor neighbourhoods. But the breakout into the mass market had
to await the 1890s, when the ABC (Aerated Bread Company) and J. Lyons and

3.23 A typical Lyons tea shop of 1907, one of as many as nine or ten on Edwardian Oxford Street. The Circus Restaurant, shown opposite, is to the left. (Historic England Archive, BL 20144)

Co. chains strewed rival tea rooms along main streets. Piccadilly was the venue for Lyons' first neat-looking tea shop (originally called a depot) in 1894; by 1900 there were 37 of them in London, and by 1910 nine on Oxford Street alone (fig. 3.24). Lyons shunned the smart trade until 1896, when its Trocadero Restaurant opened in Shaftesbury Avenue, geared to catch the post-theatre clientele; the company's famous corner houses were Edwardian afterthoughts. The tea shops put paid to the old coffee shops, just as coffee shops have obliterated tea shops in London today. They were aimed mainly at women, not least women shoppers, who had seldom been welcome even in restaurants, let alone pubs, without a male companion. The 1890s was perhaps the first decade when single

3.24 Queen's Hall, Langham Place. Exterior in 1894, with rich carving and busts of composers. T.E. Knightley, architect. (Historic England Archive, BL12575)

unaccompanied middle-class women could feel at tolerable ease on major London streets.

Finally, in this résumé of cultural facilities, halls and recital rooms for classical music. Previously, much of London's public musical life had taken place in a group of smallish halls, none dedicated to concerts alone, though a few, such as the Hanover Square Rooms and Argyll Rooms, became favoured for them. A sizeable and successful Victorian venue was the St James's Hall in Piccadilly, dating from 1858 and sponsored by music publishers, but that too was multi-purpose and lacked a presence on the street. Even larger auditoria were needed to withstand the powers of modern choirs and orchestras – and with bigger spaces and forces the acoustics could be problematic, as the Albert Hall's vexing inadequacies revealed.

These shortcomings were addressed in the Queen's Hall, Langham Place, which opened in 1893. The idea seems to have started with a music-loving solicitor, J.S. Rubinstein, who persuaded a rich and eccentric client, Francis Ravenscroft, proprietor of the Birkbeck Bank, to pay for it. The hall was rumoured to have cost the fabulous sum of £200,000. Its designer, T.E. Knightley, gave it a sumptuous curving façade in a Beaux-Arts style (fig.3.24), and an elliptical auditorium on whose acoustic profile he took advice. Built just in advance of Wallace Sabine's

3.25 Mezzo-soprano Jamie Barton and conductor Kathleen Kelly at the Wigmore Hall, Wigmore Street, 30 November 2019. (Courtesy of Alecsandra Raluca Dragoi)

pioneering research on musical acoustics, the Queen's Hall got things about right, perhaps by a fluke. It became the preferred London venue for major concerts and the original home of the Proms, inaugurated in 1895 by the great conductor Sir Henry Wood and the hall's manager, Robert Newman. The hall was burnt out in 1941 to universal regret.

On top of the Queen's Hall, there was a smaller recital room which George Bernard Shaw likened to a cigar-shaped steamer saloon. A run of small, continental-style salons for chamber music and the like also sprang up around this time, not far from the Queen's Hall. All were promoted by leading pianoforte firms – mostly foreign concerns that had recently risen above the ruck of English mid-century piano makers – and were combined with their showrooms. The first was the London counterpart to New York's Steinway Hall, created by converting some existing premises in 1878. Later examples were purpose-built. Two such were the private Brinsmead Hall, tucked at the back of a Wigmore Street address, and the Salle Erard above that firm's showroom in Great Marlborough Street – both have now gone. Finally, back in Wigmore Street came that blessed survival, the Wigmore Hall, opened in 1901 (fig.3.25). It completed a building programme started ten years before by the German piano makers Bechstein and was known as the Bechstein Hall until that firm's unjust expulsion during the First World War.

At the other end of the leisure spectrum comes sport. Outdoor sports had been on the rise in London for at least thirty years, as Sundays became secularised and leisure time lengthened. Tennis, golf, cricket, rowing, swimming, running, cycling, boxing, rugby football and soccer were all in vogue by 1890. Some of these sports had long been popular; others had acquired rules and organisation only recently. Much of this sporting activity took place perforce in the public parks, which were becoming oversubscribed. The parks had been created for strolling decorously around in, and that is how they were still mostly used. The naturalist W.H. Hudson claimed that over 100,000 had visited Southwark Park one day, although 'the atmosphere is laden with smoke, and everything that meets the eye, even the leaves and grass, is begrimed with soot'.

But many park visitors were more active now and needed catering for. In Hackney's Victoria Park, famous for its political rallies, an astounding '25,000 persons had been counted as bathing between 4 a.m. and 8 a.m. on a Sunday morning' in 1890. The London County Council as the main parks authority was urged to create a similar swimming lake in Finsbury Park. That park already possessed an enclosed cricket ground but as yet no pavilion or dressing facilities. Instead, the LCC added tennis courts, and from 1893 it registered ballboys for hire and provided posts to which players had to attach their own nets. Learning to cycle became a craze in the 1890s (fig.3.26), and in Battersea Park tenders were invited for hiring out the machines. Cricket was also popular there, John Burns being a frequent participant. By 1901 the LCC had erected 22 bandstands in its parks and was sponsoring four bands. Municipally equipped leisure facilities were widening the whole time.

To meet this surge in demand a number of recreation grounds came into being to supplement the parks. A pioneer was the Paddington Recreation Ground of 27 acres, enlarged from a private cricket ground and opened to the public in 1888. Quintin Hogg's Regent Street Polytechnic held its outdoor sporting events at Paddington, until these activities emigrated to Chiswick in 1906. The Polytechnic sponsored a broad range of amateur sports clubs, in accordance with its muscular Christian ethic of hard work, hard play and temperance. Its men's athletic, rambling, boxing, football and cycling clubs were already thriving by 1890. Now women students at the Polytechnic and beyond were joining in and asserting their sporting rights too, to be teased in the last of the Gilbert and Sullivan operas, *Utopia Limited*, premiered in 1893:

With a ten-mile spin she stretches her limbs,
She golfs, she punts, she rows, she swims.

3.26 Weekend cycling in Battersea Park. (J.J. Sexby, *The Municipal Parks, Gardens, and Open Spaces of London*, 1905)

London football meanwhile was going professional at the top, by a trend percolating down from the North. Royal Arsenal was the first London team to do so, in 1891. As Woolwich Arsenal, the club soon joined the North- and Midlands-based Football League. Other London clubs that turned professional preferred the rival Southern League started in 1894 by Millwall Athletic, for instance Tottenham Hotspur, Fulham and Thames Ironworks (later West Ham).

The early clubs shifted quixotically from one ground to another. Arsenal occupied four different homes around Plumstead before settling in 1893 at the Manor Ground. Queen's Park Rangers may have played at nearly twenty different grounds between 1889 and 1917. Millwall occupied a 420 by 400 ft patch of muddy ground on the Isle of Dogs next to the Millwall Docks between 1890 and 1901. Most spectators stood behind a picket fence, but there was one makeshift stand, to which a second was added later. Fulham, the rare exception of stability, moved to Craven Cottage in 1896 and has stayed there ever since.

Thames Ironworks (West Ham) has the most intriguing early history. The team was started off and sponsored by Arnold Hills, managing director of the Thames Ironworks. Sportsman, teetotaller and vegetarian, Hills saw football as a means to improving employer-employee relations after a bitter strike. The side (fig.3.27) began life in 1895 on a site near the works at Canning Town, playing on a pitch encircled by a cinder cycle track, drainage trenches and canvas sheeting to stop spectators looking in without paying. Exceptionally, the ground boasted floodlighting from the start, presumably by arc lamps. But Hills soon moved the club to the Memorial Ground at Plaistow, for which he paid personally. The stadium had a capacity of 100,000 spectators and boasted a cycle track, running track, tennis courts and large outdoor swimming pool over and above the football pitch. Hills even contrived to have the present West Ham Station built next to the ground (opened 1901). But tensions developed. Hills wanted the club to stay amateur and attached to his firm, but the team's directors and players saw professionalism as the only way to fill the ambitious grounds. Nor was the Memorial Ground easy to reach for the workers of West Ham, the team's natural supporters. The upshot was that the club changed its name in 1900 from Thames Ironworks to West Ham United, was expelled from the Memorial Ground by Hills and moved to Upton Park in 1904, where it flourished.

There are no trustworthy estimates for attendances at the early professional football matches. Tickets for West Ham matches cost fourpence in 1897–8, or five shillings for a season ticket. For Football League matches, the view is that most spectators came from the skilled working and lower middle classes, not all by any means young. Manchester United attracted between 10,000 and 20,000 spectators per match in the 1890s. London crowds were probably smaller but growing. For FA Cup finals we have reliable figures: 32,810 at the Kennington Oval in 1892; and then rising attendances at the Crystal Palace, where the final was subsequently played, from 42,560 in 1895 to 73,833 in 1899.

* * *

Whether at sporting events, music halls or just in the streets, people were now behaving themselves better in public. There was less roistering, drunkenness and street brawling than in Georgian or early Victorian urban life. The Londoner, recalled the journalist George R. Sims, thinking of nights in the West End, 'was becoming less insular and more cosmopolitan in his tastes, and he was gradually learning to enjoy himself without the display of exuberant animal spirits'. This helped ease the constraints on women and allowed them to take a fuller part in public life.

Better education, better policing, better government and the campaigns of the temperance movement all played some part in this change. Another contributor was the spread of information of all kinds through the cheap press. No less than 200 new periodicals were launched nationally in 1888. Most were ephemeral, but one such led to the so-called Harmsworth revolution – the last great leap in the rampant expansion of the Victorian newspaper industry.

The London printing industry sprawled far and wide over the western and north-western outliers of the City. But it was in and around Fleet Street and the Strand that most national newspapers and magazines had clustered. Many still occupied adapted, rickety premises. *Cycling*, one of the new sporting magazines, was produced from an old house in Bouverie Street on presses powered by a beam engine in the basement. 'Every time *Cycling* went to press,' recalled an employee, 'with its rapidly increasing circulation making ever more drastic demands upon the machinery, the building used to rock and sway.'

Alfred Harmsworth started out with publications of the same kind, popularised by a hunger for easy reading among the newly literate classes. He began as a juvenile editor for *Youth* and *Bicycling News* before plunging into proprietorship in 1888 with *Answers to Correspondents*, modelled on George Newnes's circulation-busting *Tit-Bits*. Alfred provided the drive and ideas, his canny brother Harold the financial control. Boosted by prizes and games, the circulation

3.28 Carmelite House, Carmelite and Tallis Streets, City of London, built for Alfred Harmsworth's Associated Newspapers in 1898. View of 1974. (Collage 38636)

of *Answers* had reached 200,000 by 1890. *Comic Cuts* and *Illustrated Chips*, nothing more than collections of jokes, followed on. Together they laid the foundations of the vast Harmsworth fortune, which Alfred spread generously around his large family. In 1894, he bought his first newspaper, the ailing *Evening News*, and turned it around. Two years later, after months of careful rehearsals and investment, he launched the *Daily Mail* with an unprecedented opening print run of 200,000. It has been the most consistently resilient of modern London newspapers. After that came the *Daily Mirror*, launched in 1903 as a paper written by and for women. When the women failed to respond, Harmsworth dropped the price, broadened its appeal, brought in photographic illustrations – the paper's main selling point – and slowly dragged the *Mirror* into profit.

Harmsworth succeeded not because he was original but because he was organised (with brother Harold's help) and ruthless. When he brought his first little empire together in Tudor Street south of Fleet Street, his room was at the top of a steep stair which, he used to say, 'makes it easier for me to kick people down'. This brashness marked him out as Britain's first modern newspaper mogul. He

3.29 Lord Harmsworth's office at Carmelite House.

also cottoned on to changing conditions and technology. The release of a swathe of property south of Fleet Street after the City Corporation redeveloped its old gasworks allowed up-to-date printing and newspaper buildings to be erected. Carmelite House, commissioned by Harmsworth for one of these sites as the headquarters of the *Daily Mail* and opened in 1899 (fig.3.28), was designed for American-style efficiency, with a special suite for journalists, a telegraph room in one corner and a private roadway for fast delivery of newsprint and dispatch of the finished papers. There was no boardroom or library, only a fancy room for Harmsworth himself (fig.3.29). The compositors on top of Carmelite House were equipped with Ottmar Mergenthaler's Linotype machine, an American innovation introduced to England in 1891. Linotypes revolutionised composition and, together with the fast-speed lines of rotary presses thundering in the basements, opened the way to the mass-circulation newspaper.

Improved policing may also have contributed to greater public calm. It is often imagined that in late Victorian times there was a policeman on every London street corner, especially at night. But police numbers had risen only in proportion to population, from 3,000 for one and a half million inhabitants within the Metropolitan Police District when the force was formed in 1829, to 16,000 for seven million in 1899. Official figures show a sustained drop in reported crime during the 1880s, allowing the Commissioner, Sir Charles Warren, to claim that 'London is the safest capital in the world for life and property'. The creation in 1878 of the Criminal Investigation Department, or CID – a reform of the detective branch on Parisian lines – sharpened the force's investigative capacities. Nevertheless, the level of theft, burglary and assault, especially in poor neighbourhoods, would shock the cosseted modern Londoner.

After a period of discontent that brought the Metropolitan Police close to an outright strike, morale may have been on the ascendant after 1890, when Sir Edward Bradford took over as Commissioner. That same year the Metropolitan Police moved into fresh headquarters, the famous New Scotland Yard on the Victoria Embankment. It was the last and subtlest of Norman Shaw's London architectural character-sketches, its four-square profile and blend of stern granite and cheerful brick bespeaking a friendly fortress (fig.3.30). Many new police stations were built across the capital over the next two decades, so that the force became better housed.

* * *

Government in London changed both in structure and in people's expectations of it with the election of the first London County Council in 1889 (fig.3.31). The LCC has largely had a good press for the achievements of its early years. It came in

3.30 New Scotland Yard, the original block shortly after completion, with Victoria Embankment in front. R. Norman Shaw, architect, 1886–90.

3.31 Original seal of the London County Council, designed by Walter Crane, 1889.

just after a period of social turmoil. The hope was that the LCC would sort things out, calm things down and dispense social justice. Things did indeed quieten down. There were no major strikes and demonstrations in the 1890s, and the fear of urban revolution faded. But that was hardly due to the LCC, which for most of the decade was finding its way.

Hitherto the government of Victorian London had been hopelessly balkanised. In theory the City and umpteen parish vestries ran their own patches. But a cluster of bodies such as Poor Law unions and school boards had been imposed on top of them to grapple with London-wide issues, headed by the Metropolitan Board of Works. The LCC had been created as a hasty afterthought to the Local Government Act of 1888 which established county councils and county boroughs. When it took over from the Board of Works, it inherited its headquarters, staff and powers – but little more. The vestries and most of the overlapping special bodies were still there. To do anything original, the LCC had to promote new legislation in Parliament and raise the money.

What was actually being achieved on the ground by public bodies in London during the 1890s? To answer that, it is best to start not with housing but with baths, libraries and schools. Libraries are among the success stories of the '90s. It had been permissible to build municipal libraries since the 1850s, but the vestries lacked the funds, and the mass of the population was too illiterate. Board-school education changed that. From the late 1880s, the wealthier vestries started to provide libraries, while philanthropists succoured poorer districts. The first big benefactor was John Passmore Edwards, a self-educated Cornishman with reformist and temperance credentials who owned a string of newspapers and journals. The Passmore Edwards libraries in Southwark, Tottenham, West Ham and elsewhere were often attractively designed. Later came larger ones, some subsidised by the American plutocrat Andrew Carnegie (fig.3.32).

These libraries did not at first operate in the open way they do today. The accessible part usually consisted of rooms for reading newspapers and reference books (fig.3.33). If you wanted to borrow a book, someone had to get it for you. There were complex catalogue systems to achieve this, including a bulky device called the Cotgreave Indicator, invented by the borough librarian of West Ham. The open lending library with the borrower taking books off the shelves appears to have been pioneered in Croydon at the end of the 1890s.

3.32 Carnegie Library, Shepherd's Bush Road, Hammersmith. H.T. Hare, architect, 1905. One of the second generation of municipal public libraries. (Historic England Archive, BL19188)

3.33 Newsroom at St George's Public Library, Buckingham Palace Road, Westminster, 1894. Early public libraries encouraged the reading of newspapers. (Historic England Archive, BL12809)

Municipal swimming baths were another advance of the time. Once again it was the maligned vestries that pioneered them. As with libraries, they had had powers to build baths since the 1850s, but in the early examples sanitary aims prevailed, so cleanliness and laundry facilities were the main goal. The new baths of the 1890s (figs 3.34, 3.35) were largely about swimming – the kind of popular and 'rational' recreation of which the reformers approved. Loans from central government helped the vestries to finance them. They supplemented a ragbag of private baths previously available only to those who could afford them.

In all the above, the LCC had no hand. Nor could it yet emulate the achievement of the School Board for London. All through these years the School Board, working from imposing headquarters on the Thames Embankment, was churning out pupils, teachers and buildings. It passed through several phases. First came a desperate struggle to provide a basic minimum, then a period of sure-footed expansion. Finally, a conflict-dogged decade in the 1890s ended in bitter confrontation with the Conservative Government. The Board was brutally abolished at the end of 1903, when elementary education went to the LCC.

The School Board as an elected body preceded the LCC by almost twenty years, as we saw in Chapter 1. By 1890 it had become party-political, with the so-called Moderates opposed by the so-called Progressives (a loose alliance of left-Liberals and socialists), though the divisions were fluid. Many School Board

3.36 (above) Rosendale School, Herne Hill, built 1897–1900. A low-rise school of the type latterly favoured by the School Board for London. (Rosendale School)

3.34, 3.35 (above left) Lambeth Baths, Lambeth and Kennington Roads. A. Hessell Tiltman, architect, 1896–7. Exterior and men's first-class swimming baths. The baths were destroyed by a flying bomb in 1945, which killed 37 people. (Lambeth Landmark, SP12/537/23 and 12/537/2)

members were socially active clergymen – low Anglican or Nonconformist – and there was an excellent system whereby members took a personal interest in their local schools.

The Board's leading light until 1897 was the Reverend J.R. Diggle, a canny political operator. A moderate Moderate, he was keen to forward the Board's work but wary about expenditure. Then Diggle fell from power. The Progressives now began egging the Board on to go faster and offer a practical education beyond the 'three Rs' – reading, writing and arithmetic – with facilities for subjects like cookery and woodwork that would prepare children for employment, and higher schools for bright children beyond the age of eleven. The novelty in board-school architecture at this time was not the strapping elementary schools on three storeys, still going up, but the single-storey annexes for practical subjects tucked around their skirts, along with a sprinkling of low-rise schools in the suburbs (fig.3.36).

By statute, the School Board was not allowed to provide secondary education. Although it found ways round this by putting on evening classes, these were close to being illegal. The simple recourse would have been to go to Parliament and acquire powers to run secondary schools. But Lord Salisbury's Conservative Government was never going to allow that, as the Tories were averse to the school boards and to the London board most of all.

It might be supposed that the LCC, which enjoyed a Progressive majority for most of the 1890s, would have supported the Board, but not so. Some of this was sheer rivalry. More rationally, the few LCC members who took an informed interest in London education, led by Sidney Webb the Fabian, believed that a root-and-branch reform was needed. Webb dreamt of a new unified system, overseen by the LCC, which would run right through from elementary to secondary schools, and then on to the new polytechnics or even universities.

The LCC got a toe into education itself from 1892, when the short-lived Liberal Government gave it powers to distribute money for vocational education in London via a new ad hoc body called the Technical Education Board. Directed by the able William Garnett, this body began to create or expand a range of technical institutes and art schools to stand alongside the infant polytechnics, from schools of nautical cookery in Stepney and photoengraving and lithography off Fleet Street, to the famous Central School of Arts and Crafts, 'a school of University rank for the artistic crafts', under the architect-teacher W.R. Lethaby (fig.3.37). Out of this initiative came also the London School of Economics, founded in 1895 to provide advanced commercial education for the capital's proliferating legion of clerks. Such training, hitherto neglected in London, was vital as office work began to dominate the metropolitan economy. Soon, however, Webb and his allies contrived to turn the infant school of economics into a kind of research institute, to the annoyance of many LCC members.

By 1900 Garnett and the Technical Education Board, with help from the independent City Parochial Foundation, had turned the jumble of polytechnics, technical institutes and art schools into something like a coherent system of higher education for London, comparable with provision in Germany and France. Once that was in place, people asked why there were two education authorities for London, not one. The solution had to await the new century, but the argument rumbled right through the 1890s and impaired relations between the LCC and the School Board.

All the same, the School Board was very effective and energetic in its day-to-day operations, never more so than in the late 1890s when it was under Progressive control. Nemesis was round the corner, but no one knew that yet. Contrast this with the early LCC, elected in 1889 without new powers, and no definite mandate except to behave like the government for all London. Debate came first, before much could be done. Between 1889 and 1892, the councillors elected themselves

3.37 Central School of Arts and Crafts, with London Day Training College to right, in 1956. Built to designs by the LCC Architect's Department, 1905–8. (Collage 199973)

a prestigious first chairman, Lord Rosebery, the future Prime Minister (fig.3.38), and talked a lot about reform.

How much they talked and how little they did can be gauged from a 600-page book devoted to the history of the first LCC administration, published with impressive immediacy by one of its Radical members in 1892. This tells us, for instance, that the members told the Council's Architect to go and find out how many swans there were in Battersea Park; they sanctioned the provision of temperance refreshments and temperance literature for an August bank holiday at Blackheath so long as the litter was cleared afterwards; and they worried about the welfare of Zaeo, a svelte trapeze artist then starring at the Royal Aquarium. The temperance and purity lobby was voluble amongst LCC Progressives, who were agitating about theatres and music halls before Mrs Ormiston Chant appeared on the scene. Salaries and pensions were also debated, as part of a drive for openness. It was agreed that the names and salaries of all LCC staff should be clearly stated and published every year – a novelty in local government.

All this fussing over minutiae betrayed the fact that there was little money to do anything new. The LCC inherited some big improvement schemes from the Metropolitan Board of Works: the completion of Rosebery Avenue, Clerkenwell, for instance, and the building of the Blackwall Tunnel. Little else was in the

3.38 The first meeting of the London County Council at Spring Gardens, Lord Rosebery standing, 1889. From a painting by Henry Jamyn Brooks. (Collage 14114)

pipeline, for financial reasons. The Board of Works' clearances and streets had largely been paid for by the tax on coal and wine coming into London – the same revenues that had paid long ago for the building of St Paul's. Latterly these had been shared between the City and the Board of Works. The Government gave notice before the LCC came into being that this could not continue, and it did not. It did get some extra government support but not much, while the chances of raising the precept or allocation it took from the local rates were slim.

So the early LCC spent a lot of time arguing for the reform of London government finance. The Progressives wanted rating to be revalued throughout the city, so that rich Conservative vestries did not connive with local owners to undervalue their properties, thus reducing the income available to the LCC via its precept. Hence began a long campaign for rating equalisation and redistribution of wealth from rich areas of London to poor ones, culminating in the 1921 rates strike in Poplar known as Poplarism. The other strategy which it was hoped would boost the LCC's ability to act was to push for property owners to contribute towards urban improvements from which they benefited financially. Compensation had always been paid when land was taken away for a street-improvement or slum-clearance scheme. But there was no mechanism for the opposite, when owners benefited from an improvement – a betterment levy, as it came to be called. The LCC Progressives chewed these issues over for years, in the hope of getting ambitious improvement schemes off the ground. They never succeeded. But there were interesting by-products of this campaign, including an attempted new land map of the whole of London showing exactly who owned what and how much it was worth – a new Magna Carta for London, as it was sometimes termed.

This delay before the LCC could set its mark on London is reflected in the Council's architecture of the early 1890s. Along the drab Rosebery Avenue, for instance (fig.3.39), the LCC built no more than a gas-meter testing station and a weights and measures office. Fire stations were the biggest things that its in-house architects were then designing, and to start with these were just like those of the Board of Works. Not until the end of the decade did the first of the brilliant Arts and Crafts fire stations that transformed the look of LCC architecture appear, designed by a team under Owen Fleming.

3.39 Rosebery Avenue, western section, c.1910. Completed by the LCC in succession to the Metropolitan Board of Works in 1890, and no obvious improvement on earlier street schemes. (Survey of London)

Fleming and his colleagues famously cut their teeth on Boundary Street, the Shoreditch housing estate that embodied the LCC's ambitions in the 1890s – much the greatest thing it had yet achieved, and essentially the start of modern council housing. The other big task in the wings was the Kingsway-Aldwych improvement, but that had to be postponed to the new century. In both cases

Rosebery Square   Rosebery Avenue   E. C.

3.40 Arnold Circus, LCC
Boundary Street Estate,
Shoreditch, in 1907.
(Collage 254139)

long delays were caused by the time it took to buy up and clear properties. But
there were other factors. The LCC was cautious about picking up the powers
to build housing available to it under the Housing of the Working Classes Act
of 1890. No local authority had ever built more than the odd block of housing
before, and the financial implications of any larger undertaking were formidable.
All the same, the powers were taken up by the second-elected LCC, more radical
than the first, in 1893. Only then did able young men like Fleming flock into the
LCC's small Architect's Department. Only then too did the Council's Works
Department, founded as a direct-labour organisation in order to circumvent the
high tenders and poor workmanship of private builders, enter into its brief and
controversial heyday.

After long preparations, the Boundary Street Estate was created between
about 1896 and 1900. It was a magnificent but pyrrhic undertaking. Many more
people were cleared from the area than were housed in the new flats. What were
then deemed excessive interest payments had to be paid on the government
loans which the Council had to take out in order to finance the scheme. So the
rents were too high for the old slum tenants, who moved elsewhere; once more,
the scheme did little to eradicate slums. The LCC's Works Department built well

but slowly, and there was much pilfering from the site. As for its looks, the overall planning of Boundary Street is simple but impressive, centred on the great circus-hill created from the rubble of the old buildings at Arnold Circus (fig.3.40). The flats themselves are handsome in looks, specially the later blocks, which seem to have been mainly designed by Charles Winmill, a disciple of Philip Webb's. But the internal arrangements of the five-storey walk-up blocks largely replicated the flat plans of the better philanthropic housing companies. Those companies were still active in the 1890s, building more flats than the number erected by the LCC.

After Boundary Street the LCC built further tenement blocks, starting in 1898 with the elegant Millbank Estate on the site of the defunct Millbank Penitentiary behind the Tate Gallery. Here slums did not need to be cleared, so progress was correspondingly easier. But the Council's housing experts, including the architects, were turning against these tenement blocks. What they longed to build were cottage homes with gardens. The decade saw an explosion in these two-storey cottage flats or maisonettes with two doors side by side, one leading straight upstairs to the upper flat. Sometimes called Tyneside flats, they are to be found all over outer London from Tooting to Walthamstow, built by private developers and public bodies alike (fig.3.41). They, not blocks of flats, were arguably the cutting edge of housing in the 1890s. The LCC did build a sprinkling of low-rise housing at this time (fig.3.42), but the main drive for that came in the new century, as will be seen in Chapter 4.

By the end of the century both the School Board and the LCC had exasperated the Salisbury administration – a pattern consistently to be repeated in political relations between London and central government. The Conservative Government now contrived to take down the LCC by several pegs while reforming the London vestry system, which had become very uneven and overburdened. The process whereby this happened was long and contorted, going back to a Royal Commission of 1893–4, which recommended that the City and the LCC should be amalgamated. Anything that rational was never going to happen while the City wielded any political muscle. Once the Tories returned to power in 1895, it became clear, writes John Davis, the leading authority on the topic, that 'Salisbury and Chamberlain aimed at the political emasculation of Progressivism, and saw the emasculation of the Council as a means to that end'. The best argument against the LCC was that it cost a lot of ratepayers' money. Only the richer vestries showed much interest in changing current arrangements, in the hope that the contributions they paid over to the poorer districts might be reduced. Various botched proposals followed. Finally, under an Act of 1899, the vestries were reconstituted as metropolitan boroughs,

3.41 (above) Cottage flats of c.1903, Joubert Street, Latchmere Estate, Battersea. (Historic England Archive, DP105412)

3.42 (below) Idenden Cottages, Blackwall Tunnel Approach, East Greenwich peninsula. LCC cottage housing of c.1893. Now demolished.

3.43 Clerkenwell Vestry Hall (after 1900 Finsbury Town Hall). W.C. Evans-Vaughan, architect, 1894–5. (Islington Local History Centre)

a few the same size as before, more an amalgamation of several previous bodies. This borough system, which came into existence in 1900 and lasted until 1965, gave fresh powers and vigour to the lower tier of London government, counterbalancing the LCC.

That is why so many of the town halls of London are Edwardian. But as the scope of municipal activity widened in the 1890s, a few vestries had already rebuilt. Battersea was one such. Having recovered its independence in 1888, it was keen to vaunt its pride and vigour, and built what it explicitly called its 'town hall' in 1892–3. Another was Clerkenwell, which allegedly had 'the smallest and worst Vestry Hall in London' but dilly-dallied over sites for decades before plumping for one on the new Rosebery Avenue. Hardly had its vestry hall been completed (fig.3.43) before the 1899 Act pushed Clerkenwell into the embrace of Finsbury. Modestly extended, the new building became Finsbury Town Hall.

* * *

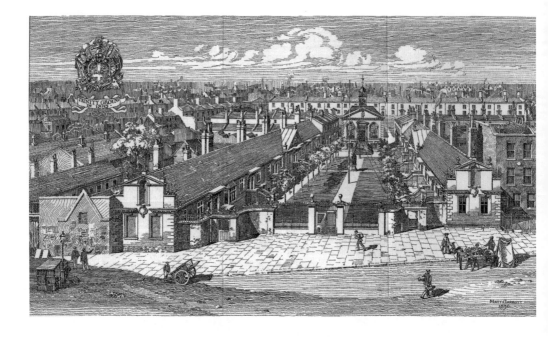

Buildings of such magnitude aimed at architecture, with which this chapter can conclude. The 1890s were an exciting decade artistically in Britain and throughout the Western world. Yet London's urban architecture of the time disappoints as a whole. Much of it is a hangover from the Queen Anne of two decades before. That is true not only of the pubs but also of the new generation of luxury hotels like Claridge's, the Connaught and the Savoy, many shops and flats lining the main arteries, and even of the LCC's earlier blocks at Boundary Street.

3.44 Trinity Almshouses, Mile End Road, drawn by Matthew Garbutt, 1896. Pull-out illustration to C.R. Ashbee's pioneering monograph on these almshouses, which led to the founding of the Survey of London.

Just then the Arts and Crafts Movement was coming to fruition. The relationship of this celebrated movement, so hard to define, with London was problematic. Its camaraderie and its production networks relied upon towns and cities, yet it was emotionally directed towards the countryside. Arts and Crafts men and women tend to be urban refuseniks. They shun London's scale, its brutality and coarseness, its capitalistic labour relations, its methods of building and its contempt for the past. The city corrupts the values and morals bound up in the best and most hallowed old architecture, they believe.

Take the example of one of the movement's ideologues, C.R. Ashbee, founder of the Guild of Handicraft – part artistic workshop, part community – at Mile End. In 1895–6 Ashbee starts a successful campaign to save a set of almshouses nearby, still doing their old and charitable job, from destruction by modern London housing (fig.3.44). He then goes on to found the Survey of London, a series of books originally intended to list all the capital's worthwhile old buildings – not on some abstract standard of aesthetic excellence, but so that they could survive as a corrective to the debased architectural priorities of the day. That was too much to ask. The Survey was soon diverted into the humbler ends of recording London's best buildings. As for Ashbee, he withdrew his Guild from the East End to small-town Chipping Campden in 1902. Yet he was quickly back. Much though Arts and Crafts folk might gripe about London, they needed it.

The leading Arts and Crafts designers tend to be marginal to metropolitan architecture during the 1890s. The exceptions are modest in number and scale. The Passmore Edwards Settlement in Tavistock Place, Bloomsbury, promoted by Mrs Humphry Ward and designed by two young architects, Cecil Brewer and Arthur Dunbar Smith, is one of them – the finest building to come out of the settlement movement (fig.3.45). Architects with Arts and Crafts sympathies certainly built a few fine London townhouses. In the suburbs there were more.

3.45 Passmore Edwards Settlement (later Mary Ward House), Tavistock Place, Bloomsbury. Smith and Brewer, architects, 1895–7. The handsome fruit of Mrs Humphry Ward's putting her money where her mouth was. (Geoff Brandwood)

Ernest Newton, for instance, designed an outstanding set of mellow houses for the builder William Willett the younger and others around Bickley and Chislehurst. Willett, a promoter of high housing standards, continued the idiom with developments in the inner suburbs at Elsworthy Road, Primrose Hill (fig.3.46), and at Eton Avenue, Belsize Park. Here Arts and Crafts architecture made a larger impact. But the creators and clients for such homes probably liked to think of them as semi-rural.

A good place to see townhouses of the 1890s touched by the Arts and Crafts Movement is towards the west end of Mount Street in Mayfair, on the posh Grosvenor Estate. Here can be found some fetching red-brick blocks and stabling by Balfour and Turner, in other words the Estate's surveyor Eustace Balfour and his partner Thackeray Turner. Even here there are nuances still of Queen Anne, merging into Georgian. Yet at the grandest level these fine architects could not measure up. Their elaborate Aldford House of 1894–7, built in Park Lane for Alfred Beit – classiest of the 'Randlords' who cleaned up during the stock market's 'Kaffir boom' in South African gold shares – was more eccentric than imposing (fig.3.48). Happier is Fairfax Wade's house for Lord Windsor, constructed in 1896–9, a plush Mayfair palazzo that balances pomp with Arts and Crafts touches (fig.3.47). But all these houses look cautious compared with the boldest of their counterparts going up around the same time in Brussels or Chicago, Vienna or Moscow. They hold back in some way; they betray some abhorrence of urban vitality. While there was an Art Nouveau vision for many cities around 1900, that did not work for London. The talent and energy were directed elsewhere.

3.46 Houses in Elsworthy Road, Primrose Hill, built around 1900 by the Willett building firm to designs by its in-house architect Amos Faulkner. The full panoply of the vernacular revival is deployed not so far from the city centre.

146

Public buildings were too big and formal for the Arts and Crafts Movement, though they often borrowed from it by way of sculpture and ornament. The great public project of the decade should have been the Victoria and Albert Museum, but though the competition, won by Aston Webb, was held in 1891, nothing happened on the ground till 1899. The result, externally at least, disappointed many. Yet there were a few masterpieces, and this chapter ends with two of them – a famous church and a less well-known public building in the outer East End.

Westminster Cathedral (fig.3.49) was built in an astonishingly short time for so grandiose an enterprise – between 1895 and 1903. That was because the client, Cardinal Herbert Vaughan, knew what he wanted. There was to be none of the usual fuss about a competition; Vaughan just chose the experienced and loyal Catholic architect, J.F. Bentley. To avoid competition with Westminster Abbey at the other end of Victoria Street, the style had not to be Gothic. Bentley decided the church would have to be Early Christian, and went off to Italy to work out what that might mean. Recently, there had been a few experiments with a kind of Byzantine style among those bored with the Gothic Revival, but nothing remotely on the scale of what Bentley came up with, or with its deftness in blending the old, the new, the monumental and the craftsmanlike.

If the exterior, with its Siena Cathedral-style stripes, pencil-thin campanile, sheer flanks and bulbous projections, is lively to the point of jollity, the interior is sober, lofty, awe-inspiring (fig.3.50). It is all deeply un-English, as perhaps befits a Catholic cathedral in London. The faithful are dwarfed by the domed and echoing

3.47 (below) 54 Mount Street, Mayfair. Fairfax Wade, architect, for Lord Windsor, 1896–9. (Historic England Archive, BL14416)

3.48 (below right) Aldford House, Park Lane, Mayfair. Balfour and Turner, architects, for Alfred Beit, 1894–7. Now demolished. (Historic England Archive, BL14414)

147

3.49, 3.50 Westminster Cathedral outside and inside. J.F. Bentley, architect, 1895–1903. (Geoff Brandwood)

expanses of bare brickwork – thankfully not yet covered with mosaic, though that has always been the intention. If it is art you want, not a great sacred space, there are mosaics enough in the side chapels, embellished over the years.

Gibson and Russell's West Ham Technical Institute, Library and Museum of 1895–9 sums up several of this chapter's themes. To most Londoners today West Ham means its football club. But between 1886 and 1965 it was a town in its own right, independent of the metropolis though integral with its economy. Until Second World War bombing laid it low, West Ham was London's foremost industrial

suburb. Its population, mostly emigrants from the inner East End, exploded from about 19,000 in 1851 to 128,953 in 1881 and 267,308 in 1901. The creation of the Royal Docks as part of the relentless eastward shift of Thames shipping started the surge. Factories took it up, notably chemical and gas works, stretching far up the River Lea, the increasingly polluted boundary between West Ham and London. Some of them may have migrated there to dodge London's regulations on noxious industries. As much to the point was their proximity to the Royal Docks, from which the coal to power them could be quickly and cheaply procured.

Some of West Ham's industries – ironworks at Canning Town, gasworks at Beckton and railway works at Stratford – differed from the London average by virtue of their size. That gave the trade unions and the labour movement fertile ground to work on. Will Thorne, the gas workers' leader, began his career at Beckton and eventually became a local MP. Before him, Keir Hardie was MP for West Ham South between 1892 and 1895 – the first labour representative anywhere to win a parliamentary election without Liberal support. Briefly, Labour took control of the borough in 1898, but could not sustain its hold on power. Whichever party held sway in the town hall, there was a sore legacy of irregular water supply, bad

3.51 West Ham Technical Institute. Gibson and Russell, architects, 1897–8. (Historic England Archive, BL15052)

drainage and poor housing on marshy terrain to tackle. West Ham's infrastructural problems were to persist right through the twentieth century.

All that has been studied. Less often remarked is the civic pride generated in West Ham during the early years of its independence. That is the context for the new building. The centre of Stratford, one of the two ancient nuclei of West Ham, already possessed a town hall, inherited from the old Board of Health that had governed the district before it won its independence. The municipality now wanted something better and bigger, something to serve, civilise and uplift its people. Hence the combination of technical institute, library and museum, within reach of the town hall. Money was not spared.

James Gibson, its main architect, was to become a specialist in exuberant public buildings. The West Ham Technical Institute is his first and freshest (fig.3.51). It is pointless to define the style; best just to say that the whole building revels in the restless blend of red brick and Portland stone in vogue all over London in the 1890s, not least at Westminster Cathedral. A colonnaded hall faces front along the main road, with cupolas at both ends for swagger. Lower gables, a little ham-fisted but it hardly matters, punctuate the side wings for technical instruction. At one end comes the semi-separate museum, with a dome and cupola of its own and a bronze relief over the door of the crusty donor, Passmore Edwards again, 'on a shield held by an ethereal female figure'. Everywhere there is a profusion of allegorical sculpture – the new, sensuous, French-influenced sculpture of the 1890s that is now replacing the stiff performances of mid-Victorian carvers (figs 3.52, 3.53). Truth and Beauty flank the building's main entrance; 'Knowledge is essential to freedom', reads one of the mottoes in the reference library. Here are all the vigour and optimism of the new West Ham, eager to take on the new century.

3.52, 3.53 West Ham Technical Institute, main entrance (below right) and sculpture by William Birnie Rhind.

4

London 1900–1914

To kick off, three passages from minor books by well-known authors. First, Charles Masterman's *From the Abyss*. Masterman (fig.4.1) is mainly remembered for *The Condition of England*, a 'state of the nation' survey he published in 1909 while serving as a junior minister in the Liberal Government. Its title picks up a phrase of Thomas Carlyle's about the plight of the working classes at the start of Queen Victoria's reign, and proceeds to review how things stand seventy years later. Masterman's assessment: not well enough.

From the Abyss, of 1902, is the first solo book by this sensitive idealist, whose political career eventually came to grief. Like other young men of his generation and class, Masterman went after university to live in the 'abyss' to see how he could help, taking a flat in a block dwelling in Camberwell and joining in local social, political and religious work. His account of his time there, rather over-written, boils over with the experience.

By then there had been slum literature aplenty. *From the Abyss* shuns the usual statistics and exposés of slum life to concentrate on the psychology of the herded London poor. Masterman tries to portray them from the inside, with much strained use of the first personal plural: their paganism, their passivity, their fleeting bursts of joyfulness and violence, their yearning for a better life in the 'not unbeautiful' new suburbs which they will inevitably colonise and pollute. Here is a taste of it.

There is so much of us, and the quantity so continually increases. That is our misfortune that is costing us more than all our crime. We press in from the surrounding country in incredible number; every ship discharges a multitude from alien shores; through the gates of birth streams in the countless host. The torrent never ceases, the supply is never diminished, the river is never dry. We swarm over the adjoining land, like a burst cloud in restless movement; continual mere pressure of numbers driving us into every corner, filling up every vacant niche or cranny, always treading on each other's heels, always

pressing into the place of those that have been suffocated in the swarm. We occupy factories, and workshops, and laundries, and common lodging houses. We pack ourselves into small cottages and decaying mansions, and block dwellings of gigantic and hideous architecture...

And again:

We live 'in the buildings'. Home is a word which is vanishing from our conversation. We live 'in the buildings' under compulsion; none speak of them with any feelings but contempt or derision; every family I know is 'intending to move'; to-morrow or the day after will see the desired change; each is ever balanced as about to start on a journey. Yet our close proximity does not kindle the fellow-feeling of condemned sufferers; next door neighbours are strangers to each other; in the midst of this human hive many walk solitary.

Next, an easier-going author, Ford Madox Hueffer – Ford Madox Ford as he later became (fig.4.2). In the Edwardian years, Hueffer was a jobbing literary journalist, scraping a livelihood to support his ramshackle lifestyle. Among his output is a pair of books about town and country, *The Soul of London* and *The Heart of the Country*, published in 1905 and 1906 respectively. They are unresearched impressions or sketches, classless and detached, written with an eye alert for colour and a deft turn of phrase.

In one of the earlier book's chapters, 'Roads into London', Hueffer shifts from one form of transport and one speed to the next, always on the move, gliding along, recording sights and sounds. At the outset he defines his canvas as 'psychological London' – the places where the city's spirit has permeated. These encompass the outermost suburbs, stretching perhaps as far as Brighton; the administrative county of London, artificially restricted by now; and the London of natural causes, 'the assembly of houses in the basin of the lower Thames', otherwise 'the zone of blackened trunks'. For Hueffer, each of these Londons is equally worth watching and listening to: there is no prejudice in favour of the centre. Here is one of many passages that foreshadow the dissolving aesthetic of the new century.

4.2 Ford Madox Hueffer, later Ford Madox Ford, with his daughter Katharine, c.1905.

For myself, when on a train into London, I feel almost invariably a sense of some pathos and of some poetry. To the building up of this railway, of this landscape of roofs, there went so many human lives, so much of human endeavour, so many human hopes. Small houses, like the ranks of an infinite number of regiments caught in the act of wheeling, march out upon the open country; in the mists of the distance they climb hills, and the serrated roofs look like the jagged outlines of pinewoods with, at the top, the thin spike of a church tower. The roofs come closer together; at last, in their regular furrows, they present the appearance of fields ploughed in slate, in tiles, in lead, with the deeper channels of the streets below. Certain details strike at the eye: parallel lines of white cement set diagonally in the slate courses whirl past, bewilderingly, like snow in a wind; lines of rails shoot suddenly from beneath the embankments; and, rather surprisingly, bits of black field lie in the very heart of it all, with cabbages growing, and a discoloured donkey tethered to a peg. The plain of roof tops broadens out again. Perhaps the comparative quiet fosters one's melancholy. One is behind glass as if one were gazing into the hush of a museum; one hears no street cries, no children's calls. And for me at least it is melancholy to think that hardly one of all these lives, of all these men, will leave any trace in the world.

Finally, a passage from one of John Galsworthy's lesser novels, *Fraternity*, published in 1909.

There are, say moralists, roads that lead to Hell, but it was on a road that leads to Hampstead that the two young cyclists set forth towards eleven o'clock. The difference between the character of the two destinations was soon apparent, for

4.3 Edwardian tenement housing: LCC gallery-access blocks at Preston's Road, Isle of Dogs, in 1905, marking a comedown from Boundary Street and Millbank.

whereas man taken in bulk had perhaps made Hell, Hampstead had obviously been made by the upper classes. There were trees and gardens, and instead of dark canals of sky banked by the roofs of houses and hazed with the yellow scum of London lights, the heavens spread out in a wide trembling pool. From that rampart of the town, the Spaniard's Road, two plains lay exposed to left and right; the scent of may-tree blossom had stolen up the hill; the rising moon clung to a fir-tree bough. Over the country the far stars presided, and sleep's darks wings were spread above the fields – silent, scarce breathing, lay the body of the land. But to the south, where the town, that restless head, was lying, the stars seemed to have fallen and were sown in the thousand furrows of its great grey marsh, and from the dark miasma of those streets there travelled up a rustle, a whisper, the far allurement of some deathless dancer, dragging men to watch the swirl of her black, spangled drapery, the gleam of her writhing limbs. Like the song of the sea in a shell was the murmur of that witch of motion, clasping to her the souls of men, drawing them down into a soul whom none had ever seen at rest.

It's a strange, semi-mystical passage from a haunted book. Galsworthy's cyclists, male and female cousins, are wrapped in cupboard love. The man, a young Fabian, believes that the answer to the problems of the city – poverty, ill health and crime – lies in social activism. He drags his softer-headed cousin into visiting the poor, but she finds she cannot stand it and has to escape – hence the bicycle ride. Theirs is just a subplot in the novel. Front of stage, Galsworthy (fig.4.4) gives the stories of the girl's father, her uncle and their bourgeois families, who are trying to live liberal lives in Edwardian Kensington. That requires care and consideration towards the working classes whose paths cross with theirs. But for one of the families it leads on to entanglement and disaster.

The theme of the passage, as of the whole book, is not really fraternity but restlessness. The cyclists escape to Hampstead and look down on London, 'that restless head', from the vantage point of the Spaniard's Road, representing the frontier between country and city. They cannot pass that 'rampart'. Instead they will be sucked back down again into 'that witch of motion, clasping to her the souls of men, drawing them down into a soul whom none had ever seen at rest'.

Restlessness or disturbance unites these three excerpts. Cities are never static. But in some extra sense, London after 1900 seems to be on the move anew, seething, uneasy, pregnant with change. That may seem like just a twist on the old cliché that Edwardian England represented one long doomed garden party, ripe for the cataclysm of war. But the impression can be shown to have a material basis, and one compatible with another and rosier idea, also hallowed in historical cliché – that the London of these years represents the acme of British imperial grandeur and show.

4.4 John Galsworthy, drawing by William Strang, 1903. (National Galleries of Scotland on loan, GML 1065)

* * *

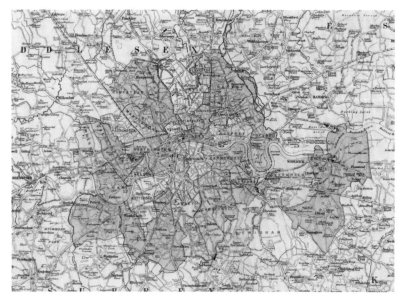

4.5 'The Environs of London showing the New Municipal Boroughs', 1902. Only the London County Council area is coloured in; outer London is shown as part of the surrounding counties. (George W. Bacon, *New Large-Scale Atlas of London & Suburbs*, 1902)

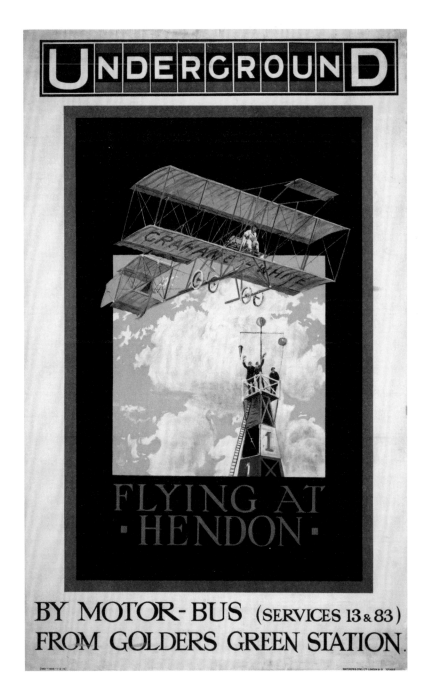

First of all, London was on the move because it had to be. Even the Victorians with their enormous stamina for walking could no longer manage London on foot. The figures may remind us of an ever-rising population dispersed over an ever-broader area. Numbers in the inner districts peak early in the reign of George V at a little under five million, while in the outer area they approximately double between 1891 and 1911 from one million or so to two million. So inner and outer London are converging in size; it is beginning to be grasped that there are not one but two Londons, distinct in government and character. The old divisions between rich districts and poor ones endure. But they are becoming overlaid with a great circumferential division, between the inner city or County of London – an area defined back in 1855 and more or less full up by the turn of the century – and a vibrant, underacknowledged outer ring beyond (fig.4.5).

Outward movement is common to all successful cities. In London, it had always been specially strong because it lacked the constraints of effective city walls, which still encircled Paris and most other European cities, or major geographical barriers like wide rivers, as in the case of Manhattan. The start of suburbanisation can hardly be pinpointed, but significant moments and periods in the process can be. The Great Fire of 1666 is one such. With the Victorians things speed up. First come the new technologies of transport, then the push to make them more widely affordable and accessible. In 1850 London has a sprinkling of railways with few suburban stops, and apart from that only horse-drawn conveyances: private carriages, cabs for hire, and a few horse-omnibus lines. By 1914, there are suburban railways, trams, buses, an underground network and automobiles; you can even fly from Hendon (fig.4.6).

Along with all that goes an ideology of dispersal. This too can be traced far back but comes to a climax after 1900. The country beyond Hampstead is depicted by Galsworthy as healthy, sane and desirable, the city below as sickly, corrupt and perilous. Combining these technologies and ideas, it now seems possible to plan and act. Planning becomes a key concept in the new century.

Taking first the means of transport, we can start with the surface railways. The Victorians had laid down the bones of a railway infrastructure, which their Edwardian descendants enriched and rationalised. With a few exceptions such as the early London Bridge to Greenwich line, the railways of both the first boom of the 1830s and '40s and its successor in the 1860s, when the companies barged across the Thames into the centre, were main-line enterprises. They were about connecting London with provincial cities, towns and seaports, with goods as much in mind as passengers. Only later did a suburban network with intermediate stops fully emerge. By and large the railway companies provided stations after

POPULATION OF LONDON

	1881	1891	1901	1911	1921
Inner London	3,910,735	4,422,340	4,670,177	4,977,741	4,936,803
Outer London	799,225	1,143,516	1,556,317	2,160,134	2,616,723
TOTAL	4,709,960	5,565,856	6,226,494	7,157,875	7,553,526

4.7 Decennial population figures for Inner and Outer London, 1881–1921

suburban communities had become established, not before. Capacity was also a problem. Suburban trains mean stopping trains, and on the two-line, up-and-down Victorian railway tracks, that spelt a headache for timetabling expresses. The companies had to be sure about their traffic to run to the costs of getting the parliamentary permission required to buy up extra land and double their tracks. On the whole they had to be nudged.

The first effective nudge was administered by the Cheap Trains Act of 1883, which applied to the Great Eastern Company. In return for permission to rebuild its Liverpool Street terminus, the company agreed to put on a number of trains for working-class commuters, so making it easier for them to migrate to the suburbs. Victorian working-class commuting by surface railway is chiefly associated with the line out from Liverpool Street. But the number and convenience of such cheap trains were limited at first. The main railway suburbs in this direction really took off only after the tracks were doubled in the late 1890s.

The Great Eastern lines and their suburban stations in the direction of Forest Gate and Ilford spearheaded a revolution in London's railway infrastructure. Soon enough, the Brighton line out of Victoria and the South Western out of Waterloo were doubled and even tripled, leading to the extension of both termini and the rebuilding of Clapham Junction where they come together (fig.4.8), as well as of many other stations along their routes. The Brighton even started to electrify in the Edwardian years, the first of London's surface railways to do so. That boundless sea of gleaming lines all the way from London Bridge to New Cross is largely Edwardian too. Even the venerable Great Western widened its tracks, adding in commuter stops and services, extra platforms at Paddington and a series of mighty steel bridges beyond to span the gulf in which Brunel had sunk the original station (fig. 4.9).

All this reflects the emergence of a hectic rivalry in commuter transport involving railways above and below ground, buses and trams, propelled by a

4.8 Aerial view of Clapham Junction Station (foreground), with railway tracks to its east,
in 2009. The station was rebuilt in 1904–10 following the Edwardian widening of the lines.
(Historic England Archive, 26452-002)

double transformation in the means of locomotion. Broadly speaking, electric traction runs ten to fifteen years in advance of motorisation. The former holds the key to the transport revolution. Only a dozen years elapse between the first public manifestations of practical electricity in London in the guise of street lighting, and the opening in 1890 of the world's first deep-level tube, the pioneering City and South London Railway from Stockwell (fig.4.10) to King William Street (the predecessor to Bank Station).

The technical advances in generating and transmitting electricity for transport are pioneered mainly in the United States and Germany. There they are at first mostly applied to surface-level trains and trams. In space-starved London they go underground. But it takes another ten years before the City and South London Railway gets a successor in the shape of the Central Line. The latter's promoters acquire the necessary Act as early as 1891, but repeatedly stumble in raising money until they are rescued by Sir Ernest Cassel, king of Edwardian financiers. Once the Central has opened in 1900 and shows a profit, competing tube schemes proliferate. The race is won by Underground Electric Railways of London, the so-called Combine, financed (after infighting in the City) by Charles Yerkes from Chicago and Edgar Speyer in London.

4.9 The widened approaches to Paddington Station seen from the platform in 1962, with bridge of 1906–7 over Bishop's Bridge Road. (Wikiwand/ Ben Brooksbank)

4.10 Stockwell Station on the City and South London Railway, soon after it opened in 1890. (TfL, from the London Transport Collection, 1999/20673)

The Combine's railways, constructed simultaneously and so at high cost, make up the core of the present-day Piccadilly and Bakerloo Lines and the Charing Cross branch of the Northern Line. Once they open in 1906–7, there is a rough-and-ready network: the London Underground system has been born (Figs 4.10–4.12). The tubes allow travellers to get swiftly from one central district to another for the first time, in the way we take for granted today. There are facilities for interchange where lines meet, while the livery of the Combine's faience-faced stations sets a pungent stamp on London's streetscape.

Despite the glamour of trains, above and below ground, trams and buses ferried more people around. The conversion to electricity of the horse-drawn trams (fig.4.14) mostly occurred before motor buses took over from horse buses. But the processes overlapped. Much of the modernisation of London's Edwardian infrastructure consisted of inserting plant, lines and road surfaces suitable for trams, cars and motor buses, as horse-drawn traffic dwindled. Horses, smelly, messy and requiring much upkeep, had by 1914 become all but confined to heavy work and deliveries. With their disappearance in favour of automobiles began also the sad decline of the London sparrow, which had thriven on horse-dung.

Electric trams enjoyed an Edwardian heyday. But they needed cumbersome street infrastructure, both the rails themselves and the apparatus that powered

4.11 (above) Elephant
and Castle Underground
Station (Bakerloo Line)
in 1907. The stations
designed by Leslie Green
for the UERL network
were engineered to carry
superstructure buildings.
Few acquired them from
the start, as this one
did. (Historic England
Archive, BL20042/004)

4.12 (right) Euston
Station in 1908, then the
northern terminus of the
City and South London
Railway. Advertising on
platform walls is already
going strong. (TfL, from
the London Transport
Collection, 1998/84312)

4.13 Underground Electric Railways of London, map of 1907, showing lines completed and under construction (flecked). Surface railways and Underground lines not belonging to the company, i.e., the Metropolitan, Central London, and City and South London Railways, are shown in red.

them. There was constant friction between the tram companies and the local authorities who had to maintain the roads. When the companies were forced by competition into electrification, they mostly opted for the cheap system of overhead wires, which added to ugliness in the street (fig.4.15). The London County Council had other ideas. As part of the Progressive policy of municipalisation, it began buying up the South London tram companies in the late 1890s and installing a neat but costly conduit system with a third rail hidden in a trench. These trams became central to the LCC's transport policy, which at the instigation of John Williams Benn, Chairman of the Highways Committee, embraced the ideal of dispersing the population from the centre.

The LCC trams were also integral to the Council's Kingsway-Aldwych improvement, which included an underground tunnel so that trams could run along the Embankment from Westminster Bridge, enter the tunnel near Waterloo Bridge (fig.4.16), then emerge beyond Holborn in Southampton Row. The Progressives on the LCC hoped to buy up and control the whole of London's tram system. After they lost power in 1907, that was never going to happen. So London ended up with a dual system, partly under municipal control on the south side of the Thames, mostly in private hands on the north side and in the suburbs. Historians have not been kind towards the LCC's venture into electric trams. Barker and Robbins, in their classic *History of London Transport*, dismiss the

4.14 Horse tramway on the former Woolwich and South East London Tramways line, taken over by the LCC in 1905.

4.15 (left) Opening of London United Tramways line, Ealing, 1901. This was the first electric tramway in London, powered from overhead wires. (TfL, from the London Transport Collection, 1998/89520)

4.16 (below left) Tram junction on the Embankment, 1906. An LCC tram emerges from the Kingsway tunnel and waits for another, which has scraped under the Waterloo Bridge approach. Motor taxi and four-wheeled horse carriages to left. (Collage 142085)

policy as 'a juggernaut that left the LCC effectively, and expensively, powerless over the future of London's transport'.

The same authorities pronounce the years 1904 to 1914 the 'decisive decade' in the city's transport systems, because on top of the Tube and the trams came the automobile revolution. When Queen Victoria died, the hansom cab was still dominant. There were precisely two motor taxi cabs in 1904, but 6,300 by 1910, more than the hansoms and hackney coaches put together. Likewise with motor buses: Barker and Robbins record 'hesitant beginnings' around 1900, alongside experiments with electric traction and even steam, and then a boom after 1905. The number of passengers carried on motor buses soon overtook those on horse buses (fig.4.17). Cut-throat competition meant that bus operations tended to lose money during the Edwardian decade, leading to mergers between small companies and eventually to the monopoly in London's public transport achieved between the world wars.

More buses, trams, cabs and cars caused increased congestion on the roads. Combined with the tangle of ownership, that prompted the first full inquiry into transport in London, the Royal Commission on London Traffic (1903–6). Its members garnered an array of statistics – for instance, on where the most crowded intersections really were (Marble Arch was the busiest, well above Bank, the so-called 'hub of the Empire'). But it could offer only piecemeal remedies,

4.17 (right) A motor taxi, motor bus and horse bus line up by the Royal Exchange, c.1909–10. (Historic England Archive, SAM01/02/0051)

4.18 Argyll Motors
showroom, Newman
Street, Marylebone,
c.1905. This Glasgow-
based company
overstretched itself and
failed in 1908. (National
Motor Museum)

because the political powers needed to co-ordinate London's transport system
went far beyond what Parliament would have conceded. Proponents of planning
in the new century were starting to see where the real obstructions to their quest
for order lay – not in the streets but in the legislature. It was all very well for a
visionary like H.G. Wells in the exhilarating essays of *Anticipations* (1901) to set
out a vision for fast motor roads and the dispersal of major conurbations, but a
hundred times harder to enact effective planning reforms against the obduracy
of existing interests. That was why the first such national measure, the Housing
and Town Planning Act of 1909 (the only substantive law fathered by John Burns
during his disappointing career as a minister), proved a damp squib.

London was only a minor source for the early manufacture of cars but a major
one for their display and purchase (fig.4.18). Kathryn Morrison and John Minnis's
Carscapes highlights the concentration of car showrooms in what now seem
surprising places like Long Acre (logical, in fact, because that had been a centre
of the coach-making trade) and Great Portland Street. The record of Edwardian
car makers in London is underwhelming. Perhaps the biggest enterprise was the
Clement Talbot Works off Ladbroke Grove, which began by assembling French
Clément-Bayard machines. Vauxhall Motors, still a famous name, lasted just two
years in the Wandsworth Road before decamping to Luton in 1905. But plenty of
London crafts firms took to bespoke chassis- and body-building as opposed to
engine manufacture.

A different spur to mobility was the improvement of London's river crossings. That went back to 1877, when the Metropolis Toll Bridges Act allowed all the bridges between Waterloo and Hammersmith to be freed from tolls, hitherto inhibitions to movement. The Metropolitan Board of Works rebuilt three of the upriver road bridges (Battersea, Hammersmith and Putney) in the 1880s, while most of the railway crossings were widened to accommodate the growing capacity of suburban services. Yet the half of the city's population living downriver from London Bridge, where the Thames was widest and busiest, were still without crossings for road traffic or pedestrians when the LCC started work, apart from the trivial Tower Subway between Tower Hill and Tooley Street. A first palliative was the Woolwich Free Ferry, opened in 1889, which survives to this day. There followed the mighty Tower Bridge, whose bizarre blend of modern steelwork with Scotch-Teutonic historicism instantly became a new symbol for London upon its completion in 1894 (fig.4.19). Then came four LCC projects, major and minor: road tunnels at Blackwall (opened 1897) and Rotherhithe (1908), and foot tunnels at Greenwich (1902) and Woolwich (1911). East London acquired no further Thames crossings for fifty years after that.

4.19 Tower Bridge, from a coloured postcard dispatched by a French tourist in 1907. Opened in 1894, the bridge was the City of London's sole effort of the period towards the beautification of London. (Ken Powell)

Tower Bridge, London

The new mobility had contradictory effects. On the one hand it spread people around and separated them out. On the other hand it helped to unify London, because people travelled more and identified less with their own outgrown parochial district. The creation of the new London boroughs in 1900 added to that trend. Not that there was much loyalty at the outset towards, for instance, reformed Finsbury or Stepney, entities pulled together from a patchwork of previous local authorities. From about then, districts begin to be increasingly identified not by parish or borough but by tube stops or bus termini – Tufnell Park, Shepherd's Bush, the Elephant and Castle and so forth.

Mobility also helped co-ordinate and stratify activities. Take higher education. When the London polytechnic movement took off in the 1890s, it reinforced local employment and identity: Woolwich Polytechnic for workers in the Arsenal there, or the Northampton Institute for the watchmakers of Clerkenwell. These specialisms persisted. But over time they came to be seen as faculties to which students travelled from one part of London or another, and constituents of a city-wide framework of educational provision. At its apex stood the sundry colleges of the University of London, notably the new Imperial College, created in 1907 by amalgamating South Kensington colleges in an effort to catch up with the great German technical *Hochschulen* and American institutes of technology. Without the new transport systems, all this would have been less feasible.

The Edwardian fire stations that the LCC built all round London (fig.4.20) followed the same trend. Earlier stations, with their horse-drawn engines and lookout towers, had been largely self-sufficient. Now they were connected by telephone, co-ordinated from the centre and supplied (after long and shameful prevarication) with motorised engines. They became parts of a network of fire protection, no longer a set of detached outposts.

In sports-going and even church-going, the same tendency was at work. People now crossed London to watch the teams they supported or hear the preachers they revered. Most of the church denominations, stuck with entrenched parochial or district systems and loyalties, resisted the change. The group that embraced it most readily were the Methodists. Led by good businessmen, they

4.21 Methodist Central Hall in the 1930s. Lanchester and Rickards, architects, 1905–11. (Historic England Archive, CC47/02686, Herbert Felton)

toyed with giving up their chapels in favour of central halls for large numbers of worshippers, who might travel some distance to attend. The halls could then be hired out during the week when not in use for religious purposes. The conspicuous example was the gargantuan Methodist Central Hall at Westminster, funded by the 'Million Guinea Fund' as an attempt to re-energise Wesleyanism by concentrating the faithful, and finally completed in 1911 (fig.4.21).

* * *

The outer suburbs were now absorbing much of London's energy and resources. The best guide to these modest places, Alan Jackson's *Semi-Detached London*, is mainly about the inter-war suburbs. But his early pages include a helpful chapter on two Edwardian examples, Ilford and Golders Green, from which we shall crib.

4.22 Ilford Town Hall in 1973. Benjamin Woollard, architect, 1899–1901. (Collage 148486)

Ilford is a classic railway suburb, strung out either side of the Great Eastern lines. It grew fast from 1890, when it had less than 2,000 houses, to almost 8,000 houses in 1900 and perhaps twice that number a decade later. It acquired autonomy as an urban district in 1894 and built itself a big stone-faced town hall in 1901; if not much can be said for its looks, it shows that Ilford was pleased with itself (fig.4.22).

The town's earlier districts close to the railway were perhaps never that appetising and today look hammered, but the outlying housing is better (fig.4.23). The biggest developer was Archibald Cameron Corbett, who had cut his teeth at Forest Gate, West Ham's most eligible district, before buying up land at Ilford and embarking from 1893 on four separate estates totalling almost 4,000 houses. New stations at Seven Kings and Goodmayes served these developments. Corbett, later Lord Rowallan, went on to build another 3,200 houses or so south of the river at Hither Green and Eltham between 1896 and 1908. A Presbyterian Scot, he stipulated that his estates should be drink-free and took an interest in his tenants' health and morals but did not interfere to excess. At first he sold 99-year leases on the old pattern, but after the passing of the Small Dwellings Acquisition Act in 1899 (not generally much used in England) he began offering 999-year leases or freehold sales – a sign of changing relationships between ground landlord and tenant. Corbett streets tend to be long, uniform and dull, but the houses themselves are good and solid. His developments have been labelled 'moral estates'.

Golders Green deserves more space, because it is the home of *the* suburb, as Hampstead Garden Suburb continues to be called locally. Though closer to

4.23 Two-storey terrace houses in Melbourne Road, Ilford.

London than Ilford, its growth only took off after 1907 when the Northern Line arrived. It acquired an ample scale of middle-class houses, shops and churches – originally also a big music-hall theatre and a cinema. It also boasted the famous Golders Green Crematorium (fig.4.24), London's first after the pioneer of 1878 at faraway Woking. The dead have always led the way in suburbanisation, so it is no surprise that the crematorium opened in 1902 before the Tube. But as a dependency of Hendon Urban District Council, Golders Green had no town hall.

Hampstead Garden Suburb, to the east of the Finchley Road, is one of the great Edwardian achievements, with an international reputation in its day. Its strengths derive from its limitations. In essence it is a large and well-planned satellite community or homestead for commuters – a garden suburb (the phrase was coined here), not a garden city. It is both a spin-off and a revolt from the idea of the self-sufficient garden city propounded by Ebenezer Howard.

Raymond Unwin made the first plan for the Suburb in 1905. At that date Howard's pioneer garden city at Letchworth, also laid out by Unwin, had barely started. Creating a complete town from scratch, without previous infrastructure or employment, was bound to be uphill work. By taking on the easier project of the Suburb (figs 4.25, 4.26), going to live there and leaving his partner Barry Parker behind in Letchworth, Unwin delivered an oblique vote of no confidence in Howard and the garden city. But he was a pragmatist. He had designed housing schemes for mining and factory villages before he leapt into the limelight with his plan for Letchworth; his ultimate objectives were better housing and health, not ideal communities. That was true also of Henrietta Barnett, who formulated the idea of the Suburb and led it to success; she too was pragmatic, not utopian like Howard.

It is often remarked that Hampstead Garden Suburb failed to attract the working classes who it was hoped would come and live there, using the Northern Line. In fact the 1911 national census records a fairly equal proportion of clerks and skilled manual workers among the heads of household in one of its best early streets, Asmuns Place. Factory workers were never likely to come in large numbers because of the cost of commuting. In the end, the Edwardians could not solve the economic conundrum of 'carriage versus rent', as the issue was called. The solution had to await the roll-out of subsidised council housing on a national scale after the First World War, in which Unwin was to be deeply involved.

Unwin's technical innovations at the Suburb had mainly to do with layout, at several levels. There is road layout – not so much curving picturesque-type roads as variations in length and contour, with splayed junctions and houses set across the angles; and minute attention to how road width, verge, pavement, front hedge (never wall), front garden and house frontage interrelate (figs 4.26 and 4.27). Then there are the rethought proportions between house and garden (front for flowers, back for fruit and vegetables); the combining of houses in unequal groups; their aspect; and a slew of clever small reforms in their internal planning. Not all this was invented in one fell swoop, but it was at Hampstead Garden Suburb that the Unwin revolution came together on the ground, just as it did on paper in his book *Town Planning in Practice*, published in 1909.

The Suburb is much more than Parker and Unwin: most of its houses are not to their design. There are also the empty and disappointing central square alleviated by three buildings by Edwin Lutyens; the monumental flats designed by A.J. Penty at the formal entrance from Finchley Road (fig.4.29); and hidden-away grace notes such as M.H. Baillie Scott's Waterlow Court for working women (fig.4.30). But Unwin's contribution was the decisive and masterly one. It was rapidly imitated everywhere. Ilford, for example, has one in the shape of Valentine's Park, one of many garden suburbs that got going just before the First World War but fizzled out afterwards. Nor was the Suburb wholly English, as is often assumed. The concept of a fully planned town extension, alien to British tradition, came from the example of Germany, then to the fore in that field. Penty's flats on the Finchley Road are highly Germanic, while Unwin studied the grouping of houses from precedents like picture-pretty Rothenburg as well as the Cotswolds, as the illustrations to *Town Planning in Practice* betray. The Germans too were the first to come and pay homage; imitative *Gärtenstädte* were soon sprouting on the outskirts of their towns.

Charles and Lucy Masterman visited Hampstead Garden Suburb in March 1908. Lucy's diary captures the freshness and hope it seemed at that moment to offer:

> In the afternoon he and I went by train to Hampstead and saw the garden suburb, dear little clean houses in gardens with splendid sweeps of country all round under snow. We saw a little quadrangle for maiden ladies and the nicest street was one called Asmuns Place, up a slope with two big trees in it, leading to a square with great pieces of grass in front of them. The effect of diving into the tunnel at Charing X and emerging into cleanliness and snow and country was magical. C. was fascinated and we agreed it made one nearly cry to think that Camberwell and West Ham and Peckham might all have been like that if people would only have taken thought and looked after them.

Hampstead Garden Suburb is worth comparing with the four cottage estates built during the same years by the London County Council, at Tooting, Norbury, Tottenham and Old Oak. They were the upshot of the switch in Council policy

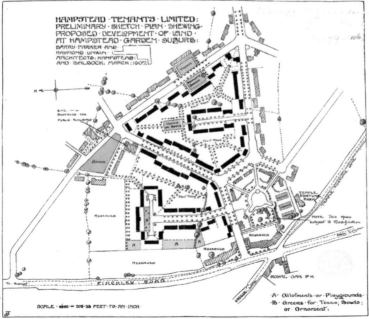

4.24 Golders Green Crematorium. Ernest George and Yeates, architects. The buildings were gradually expanded from 1902 onwards to keep pace with the crematorium's success.

4.25 Left, Hampstead Tenants' section of Hampstead Garden Suburb, as laid out by Parker and Unwin, 1907. Asmuns Place is the T-shaped cul-de-sac in the centre near the base of the map.

after 1900 towards suburban housing for the working classes instead of tenement blocks in the centre. Not that flatted estates were abandoned entirely. The LCC built several, notably the Bourne Estate in Holborn of 1905–9; some of the new borough councils followed suit; and there was a resurgence in activity by philanthropic housing trusts, some of which, including the Sutton Trust and the Samuel Lewis Trust, were new to the game. But there was a consensus that such blocks (fig.4.31) were built *faute de mieux*. Chelsea's Medical Officer of Health, for instance, reported in 1902 that the borough could only satisfy a small proportion of those who needed housing, and recommended that the rest should be left to the LCC, who would export them to the happier and healthier suburbs and bring them in by 'convenient, cheap and rapid transit to the centre'. And when, after years of slumber, the Peabody Trust took up the cudgels again around 1910, it mixed its old tenement types with some small cottage-housing developments at Dulwich and Tottenham.

4.26 (below) Typical Hampstead Tenants' cottages (British Library)

Cottages from 6/- to 15/- per week nett.

Applications of intending Tenants and Shareholders to be made to the Secretary, Hampstead Tenants Ltd., 22, Red Lion Square, W.C.

4.27 (above) Asmuns Place, Hampstead Garden Suburb, showing current state with hedges and cars partly parked on pavements. Inset, picture from Unwin's *Town Planning in Practice* of 1909, showing the original layout with deep grass verges and trees, some new and some old. The caption reads: 'A carriage drive used in place of an expensive road'.

4.28 (below) Hampstead Way, Hampstead Garden Suburb, showing treatment of verges and corner plots.

4.29 (above) Temple Fortune flats and shops, Finchley Road, at the entrance to Hampstead Garden Suburb, designed by A.J. Penty for Parker and Unwin, 1909–11.

4.30 (below left) Waterlow Court, Hampstead Garden Suburb. Flats for working women round a court, designed by M.H. Baillie Scott, 1907–9.

4.31 (below right) Beaufort Street flats for Chelsea Borough Council, 1903–4.

4.32 (above) The Prince and Princess of Wales emerge from a dwelling on the opening day of the LCC's Totterdown Fields cottage estate, Tooting, 15 May 1903. (Collage 272758)

4.33 (below) LCC Totterdown Fields cottage estate, Tooting, at Coteford Street and Blakenham Road.

4.34 LCC Old Oak cottage estate, Hammersmith, a corner in Fitzneal Street, 1912. Only a small portion of the Old Oak Estate could be built before the First World War.

The LCC had difficulty in supplying low-density houses instead of flats because there was little space left to buy and build on in the County of London. So the Council had to obtain fresh legislation that allowed it to encroach on the outer circumference beyond the county boundaries. Thus armed, it started to build from 1903. Three of its four cottage estates were planned before Hampstead Garden Suburb. Since they were for working-class tenants alone, the budgets had to be lower, the houses and gardens smaller; a certain monotony was unavoidable. The layout of the first cottage estate, Totterdown Fields, Tooting (figs 4.32 and 4.33), just prolonged the neighbouring grid of streets. But there were innovations in the grouping and details of the housing, notably improvements to the economical cottage-flat type, which the LCC believed in (but Unwin did not). Norbury and the White Hart Lane Estate at Tottenham made better use of open space. By the time the last of the four cottage estates, Old Oak at Hammersmith, was started, the LCC architects had picked up on the Parker and Unwin layouts at the Suburb. They now grouped the houses with greater deftness and variety, though always on a tight scale (fig. 4.34). Only a little of Old Oak could be built before the First World War intervened.

The growth and dispersal of London caused the LCC insuperable problems, as its need to build beyond the borders of its territory betrayed. Water supply is a good example. In the 1890s the Progressives on the Council tried several times to wrest this natural monopoly from the hands of unaccountable private companies and municipalise the whole system, as had happened in various British cities. Once again they were rebuffed by the Conservative Government, which accepted the need for reform but argued, reasonably enough, that plans for London's water required a geographical reach far beyond the LCC's area. After much bickering, the Conservatives set up the Metropolitan Water Board in 1903 on the old board-type system, with LCC nominees restricted to a minority.

Such issues led to the first calls for a Greater London government – which when it came into being in 1965 turned out by some margin less stable than the LCC. Meanwhile there was much anxiety about the Council's powers. One reason that the LCC fought the School Board so hard to take over education was that it feared marginalisation. As Laurence Gomme, the Clerk to the Council, put it, 'the Council has already lost the water supply; the Tramways and the Fire Brigade are both threatened, and the Council, if it loses Education, will be little better than a Drainage Board.' As it was, the LCC lost momentum and became more an administrative than an initiating body after 1907, when the Progressives fell from power.

* * *

4.35 Workers leaving the South Metropolitan Gasworks, Old Kent Road, c.1905. (Southwark Archives)

4.36 Siemens works, Woolwich, seen from Maryon Park in 1898. (*Siemens Magazine*, June 1927: Royal Greenwich Heritage Trust/Stewart Ash)

London in 1900 was still the biggest industrial producer in the country, with countless high chimneys belching smoke and fumes into an overcast sky. The capital's industry at this time is sometimes pictured as a medley of thousands of lowly crafts-scale firms, dwarfed by the factories of the Midlands and North. But by now there were several really large employers on London's fringes; the suburbs were far from housing alone.

Numbers of employees fluctuated. The Woolwich Arsenal was the giant, employing about 20,000 hands around 1900 at the height of the Boer War. Perhaps next in size were the railway and gas works of West Ham. Beckton Gasworks, headquarters of the Gas Light and Coke Company, is supposed to have employed 10,000 at its peak; the Great Eastern at Stratford, the biggest railway company to manufacture and service its locomotives and trains in London, about 7,000. Another big gas company was the South Metropolitan, with plants at Old Kent Road (fig.4.35) and East Greenwich and a total workforce reported as 6,000 in December 1910, though the summer figure would have been much lower. The booming gasworks are a reminder that electricity had failed to make decisive inroads on gas light and power. Numbers at the Royal Small Arms Factory at outlying Enfield Lock are given as just over 2,000 in 1893, less in 1909 – doubtless more in between during the Boer War – to shoot up again during the First World War. Back at Woolwich, varying figures are reported between 1873 and 1895 for Siemens Brothers' big telegraph and cable works, which had a front of some 700 yards along the river (fig.4.36). In some weeks during 1873, only 332 employees were present, in others as many as 2,024, depending on the state of cable contracts. But the weekly average was creeping up, to well over 1,000 in the mid-1890s.

More typical were the mid-sized factories and warehouses employing from fifty to several hundred workers apiece. In some places these were unremitting.

4.37 Hammersmith Iron Works of John and Henry Gwynne, manufacturers of centrifugal pumps, photographed by Henry Taunt, 1895. A typically sprawling riverside industrial site. (Historic England Archive, HT07065)

4.38 Lots Road Power Station in 1923. Built on the Chelsea-Fulham boundary in 1902–5 to power the UERL's trains. (TfL, from the London Transport Collection, 1999/12396)

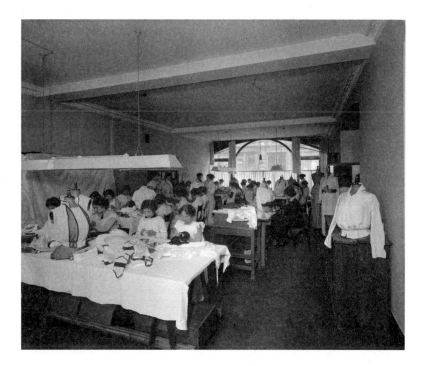

4.39 Seamstresses at Vivian Porter and Co., ladieswear and sportswear wholesalers, Holles Street, Marylebone, in 1914. The women are putting finishing touches to the garments, probably to be sold in the Oxford Street stores nearby. (Historic England Archive, BL22553)

The Thames, for instance, was blighted by mile after unsightly mile of docks, warehouses and factories (fig.4.37), stretching on the south side most of the way from Woolwich to Wandsworth with few intervals. A new break in the sequence was heralded when the LCC resolved in 1905 to build its long-sought County Hall on the unfashionable Lambeth side of Westminster Bridge. It was intended as the start of the South Bank's redemption. But industry hardly relaxed its grip on the rest of the filthy ribbon till after the Second World War.

Industries had many reasons to stay in London. The simplest was interdependence. In the East and West End clothing trades alike, the many intricate stages in finishing garments, ready-made or bespoke (fig.4.39), passed between a multitude of small firms and individuals, who had to be close together to avoid transport costs and loss of time. The same held true for the furniture trades of South Shoreditch, the subject of a model study by Joanna Smith and Ray Rogers in which the planning historian Peter Hall is quoted: 'the real assembly line ran through the streets'. For reasons of speed, newspapers were printed in the places where they were written. The first big power stations all found sites within the County of London. They could be no further removed because electricity was not yet transmissible over long distances. These included the London Electric Supply Corporation's at Deptford, the Underground Electric Railways Company's at Lots Road, Fulham (fig.4.38), and the LCC's own station at Greenwich, which supplied power for the municipal tramways. All relied on coal brought up the Thames, adding to London's pollution.

Moving production out of London to reap advantages from more space and lower costs was nothing new; the shoe and book-printing industries had long shown the way. But there were now growing numbers of escapees. Newer industries found it easiest to decamp. Vauxhall Motors' move to Luton in 1905 has been mentioned. Ferranti Ltd soon gave up trying to make its advanced electrical equipment in the capital and moved its works to Oldham in 1896 because London land prices were too high. Guglielmo Marconi founded his Wireless Telegraph and Signal Company in London in 1897 but rapidly transferred to roomy Chelmsford. The Gramophone Company, creator of His Master's Voice, emigrated to Hayes next to the Great Western line in 1907, nine years after it began. Siemens stayed partly loyal to Woolwich but moved its dynamo and motor departments to Stafford in 1904–5, after the LCC refused to exempt the firm's engineering works from the grip of its building regulations.

Clerkenwell, where there was a strong crafts tradition, 'played a crucial role in the development of London's modern precision and electrical industries', yet they exited 'very rapidly to the suburbs'. Otherwise the district's trades held up well until the inter-war Depression. True, clock- and watchmaking, once its leading industry, was in precipitate decline by 1900 because of foreign competition. Yet in 1904 the Borough of Finsbury, of which Clerkenwell made up more than half, had 10,015 workers in paper and printing; 6,021 in food, drink and tobacco; 3,979 in clothing; and 3,204 workers in metals. Only in clothing did women employees outnumber men, by almost six to one.

Many industries did not move far. Among these were the giant breweries, noxious in smell and smoke and often jammed on to constricted central sites. Usually they relocated to suburbs within reach of their city pubs. The biggest brewery amalgamation of the period took place in 1898, when three venerable companies merged to form Watney, Combe, Reid and Co. and brought production together in a giant riverside plant at Mortlake. Reid's Griffin Brewery in Clerkenwell Road now shut, to be followed in 1905 by the historic Woodyard Brewery of Combe and Co. off Long Acre. The biggest of the Shoreditch furniture firms also relocated. This was Harris Lebus, which claimed to employ over 1,000 and removed its factory out to Tottenham in 1901 in order to achieve modern single-storey 'flow-line' production instead of having to hoist heavy items up and down in old-style warehouses.

Last in this sample of centrifugalists may be mentioned the British Xylonite Company, pioneer producers of celluloid. This early plastic was invented by Alexander Parkes in Birmingham but made commercial by Daniel Spill,

who after negotiating an agreement with an American rival set up the Ivoride Works at Homerton in 1877 (fig.4.40). Basic production shifted ten years later to Brantham on the Suffolk side of the Stour estuary, convenient for import and export, but finishing of popular items like celluloid collars and combs continued at Homerton until 1897. Then, to gain space, the London factory moved out to Highams Park, just beyond what is now the North Circular Road. Here the firm made a majority of the world's ping-pong balls until its demise in 1971.

Docks and dock labour were in sorry shape during the Edwardian period except at Tilbury – beyond the boundary of London by any but an economic definition. The gains of the 1889 strike had not been maintained. Most labour was still casual and even after amalgamations the dock companies could ill afford the investment to accommodate the growing size of ships. A Royal Commission with strong City representation tussled with these issues for two years from 1900. The subsequent Bill failed in Parliament, mainly because no one wanted to pay for the proposals. The LCC next put forward its own Bill to municipalise the docks, but as usual the Conservative Government and the City wanted none of it. Finally, a compromise scheme brought the Port of London Authority into being in 1909 to buy out existing interests. It did some good work, rescued the Royal Docks and extended Tilbury, but could not reverse the underlying trend.

An article of 1903 attributed the decline of dock warehousing, especially for goods in international transit, to what we nowadays call the 'just in time' supply

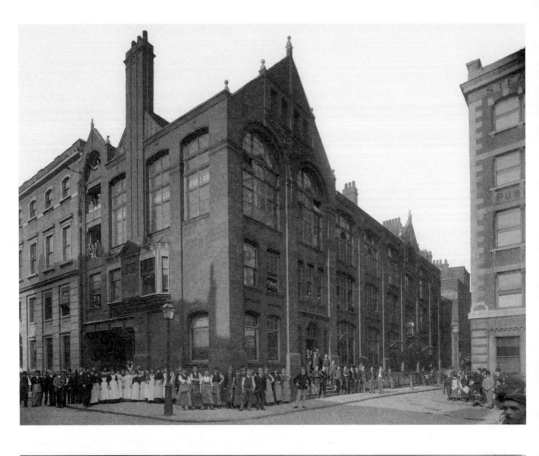

4.41 New warehouse
and workforce of
Evans, Sons and Co.,
manufacturing and
wholesale chemists and
druggists, Bartholomew
Close, City of London,
1891. (Historic England
Archive, BL11065)

chain. The railway and the steamship lessened the demand for storage, argued the author: 'the telegraph abolished the need altogether, for since an order to buy can be sent to any part of the world in a few hours, and the order can be executed so quickly . . . it is no longer necessary to incur the cost of keeping vast stocks in expensive warehouses'.

Other types of warehouse were holding their own. In the City – as yet far from a financial monoculture – the district north of Cheapside and east of Aldersgate Street was home to hundreds of warehouses that combined manufacturing, finishing, packing and dispatching with storage (figs 4.41 and 4.42). Cold stores, mainly for meat from the Antipodes and South America, were also growing in sophistication and size. Confined at first to the docks, by 1900 they were invading the streets north of Smithfield Market. Another booming genre was the monumental storage depository, linked to furniture firms or department stores. Hampton and Sons of Pall Mall built one just off Queenstown Road, Battersea, in 1900–3, conspicuous still from the railway; Whiteleys of Bayswater created a whole complex visible from the Talgarth Road; and Harrods, not content with destroying the amenity of Trevor Square near the store with a six-storey depot, in 1913–14 erected an immense depository-township on the Thames near Hammersmith Bridge (fig.4.43). Another example is the bulky Interchange Warehouse of 1901–5 at Camden Lock for storing goods moving between road, railway and canal, replacing an earlier shed on the site. Structural steel and, increasingly, reinforced concrete would have been deployed in most such buildings, hidden behind brick or terracotta fronts.

This storage capacity entailed an inexorable rise in paper transactions, as did everything to do with commerce, money and administration. That meant more clerks. The banks and insurance companies added to their staffs and rebuilt to accommodate them. The Prudential Assurance housed over 2,000 staff in its overweening headquarters at Holborn Bars in 1911. The Railway Clearing House next to Euston, which allocated money received in fares and fees between the different companies, employed 2,500 in its central office in 1914. The LCC

4.42 Inspection of
Aertex shirts by top
hats at Fore Street, City
of London, in 1901. The
shirts were made in
Nottinghamshire by
the Cellular Clothing
Company and distributed
from London. (Historic
England Archive,
BL16777)

employed 3,700 staff in 1891, but that had more than doubled by 1911, which was one of the prime reasons for building County Hall. Further increases in central and local government staffs followed the Liberals' employment and social-security reforms. Cornwall House in Stamford Street, Waterloo, built for the Stationery Office in 1912–15 (fig.4.44), is said to have been commissioned to cope with the paperwork needed to manage the new national pensions and insurance systems. As yet there was no thought of sending government clerks to the suburbs. That had to await the 1920s, when the Ministry of Pensions was relegated to Acton.

White-collar workers – clerks in the terminology of the time – made up the majority of Edwardian commuters, coming in from the suburbs to run the commerce of the City of London and staff the banks, the civil service, the sundry administrative boards and bodies, the railway bureaucracies, the law and accountancy firms and all manner of other concerns (fig.4.45). At the heart of this clerkly world lay the City, now at the arrogant acme of its power. Some figures give the outline. 27,000 people lived in the City in 1901, almost half the number of twenty years before. But 332,000 worked there every weekday (Saturdays included), rising to 364,000 in 1911. Membership of the Stock Exchange peaked at 5,567 in 1905. Rush hour was more brutal than today.

> Crowds bubble intermittently from the underground stations. 'Buses in endless procession converge upon the Bank. The pavements are black with people. The scene from the Mansion House steps beggars description. You look upon a very maelstrom of men ... During an hour these multitudes in drab march past to the relentless City, to barter what they have of value for their daily bread.

The author of that excerpt from George R. Sims' *Living London* was thinking of the toiling mass of clerks. Above them were the managers and bankers, who might arrive later by hansom cab or brougham – though Sir Ernest Cassel made do with the Central Line which he had financed.

4.43 (above) The former Harrods Furniture Depository, Barnes. (Wikipedia/Henry Kellner)

4.44 (above right) Cornwall House, Stamford Street, Waterloo. Built for the Stationery Office in a candid reinforced-concrete idiom by the Office of Works in 1912–15, it was taken over as a military hospital for the duration of the First World War. (Wikipedia)

4.45 (right) Clerks at the Caslon type foundry, Chiswell Street, Barbican, 1902. A solitary woman in the centre is seated at an adding machine; the surrounding men stand or perch on stools. (St Bride Printing Library)

The City was at the black heart of London's restlessness. On the Stock Exchange (fig.4.46), vividly chronicled by David Kynaston, frenetic transactions alternated with bouts of indolence and boisterous games. The Boer War roused the brokers and jobbers to patriotic excesses, such as rousing choruses of the national anthem when Mafeking was relieved. There were sporadic bloodlettings, when cocky financiers who had made their millions doubtfully and spent lavishly got their comeuppance. The most sensational came in 1904, when the playboy company promoter Whitaker Wright was convicted of fraud and committed suicide with a cyanide pill before he could be removed from the Old Bailey.

Few brokers or jobbers on the Stock Market thought much about the longer term, the wider national interest or, as was becoming painfully clear, industrial investment. All that was left to the elite in the banking community. Yet the market was a major cog in London's whole financial system, which played a crucial role in national prosperity. Kynaston sums it up:

4.46 (above)
'"Hammering" a Member': drawing by Arthur Buckland from Godefroi Drew Ingall's essay on the Stock Exchange in George R. Sims, *Living London*, vol. 1 (1901).

> As the world's only free gold market, it offered a unique attraction to overseas depositors; it was the centre of international banking; bills of exchange drawn on London financed most of the world's trade; its capital market raised almost half the world's total exported capital; it remained the main market for insurance, many commodities, and such specialist activities as the chartering of ships. The City was, in short, as much as ever the indispensable place.

Even so, there were symptoms of anxiety and vulnerability. American finance had heavily underwritten the loans needed to pay for the Boer War and the Tube; and the main stock-market panic of these years, in 1907, derived from the collapse of the Knickerbocker Trust in New York. American investment, know-how and

4.47 (below) The former
Howard de Walden
Nurses' Home and
Club, Langham Street,
Marylebone. Built in
1899–1900 and mainly
paid for by Lady Howard
de Walden to assist a
campaign to improve
conditions for private
nurses. Now a hotel.
(Chris Redgrave)

habits were all starting to penetrate London life, as part of a wider shift towards so-called cosmopolitanism – the more blatant role of money and business in high society, and specifically the increasing penetration and acceptability of Jews in high finance. Feared by many, the trend was welcomed by others. The young Winston Churchill, according to Beatrice Webb's diary, regarded the 'cosmopolitan financier' as 'the professional peacemaker of the modern world, and to his mind the acme of civilisation'.

In the humbler white-collar world, concern begins to be felt in the Edwardian period about the pay and career prospects of male clerks in particular, and trade unions or staff associations to represent them make headway. In the bigger offices a dual labour market emerges. Career paths open up for clerks with good skills, while professional qualifications can be earned through the commercial education courses now increasingly available, from the London School of

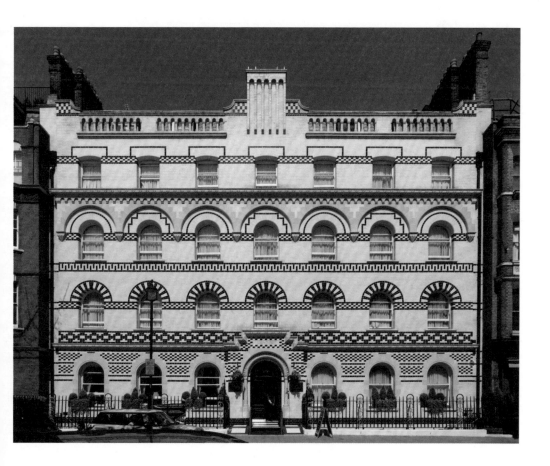

Economics downwards. At the lower end of the market, women start to take over routine office tasks like typing and telephony, adding to roles they have long been filling in the job market as nurses, shop assistants and cleaners. They amount to between 20 and 25 per cent of London's clerical workers in 1911.

Most of the women in office employment were living at home and commuting. But for a growing number, especially young girls from the provinces, home meant hostels and halls of residence. Charities such as the Young Women's Christian Association had for some time been commandeering houses to accommodate and shelter single women, but now purpose-built hostels were going up in increasing numbers. A clutch appeared in the streets behind Westminster Cathedral, another in Marylebone north of Mortimer Street. They varied in quality from just above a doss house to the level of a women's club.

Some were hostels for specific employments such as nurses and shop assistants. The Howard de Walden Nurses' Home and Club of 1900 in Langham Street, Marylebone, faced in shiny-white sanitary ware, is a conspicuous example (fig.4.47). Shop girls hitherto had been treated like maidservants and jammed into dormitories over Victorian shops. In one of the new Marylebone hostels, girls working at John Lewis were housed two to a room with provision for eating and relaxing though, no doubt, strict rules about visitors. More generous were Messrs Bourne and Hollingsworth, who took their obligations in loco parentis to heart, providing fuller facilities for employees of their Oxford Street department store in two hostels opened in Gower Street and Store Street just before the First World War.

By then, dedicated accommodation for shop girls was looking anachronistic. Gordon Selfridge provided none when he opened his own ambitious Oxford Street store in 1909. The same move towards letting staff live their own lives and find their own housing was at work in domestic service. There were still over 200,000 full-time servants in London on the eve of the war, not that many less than forty years before, but fewer of them lived in. Many middle-class households made do with just one indoor servant, almost always female.

Edwardian novels are full of solitary women buffeted by the brutalities of working and living in London, for instance Horace Newte's Sparrows: The Story of an Unprotected Girl, and H.G. Wells's Ann Veronica, both of 1909. Many doctors and health specialists, along with the eugenicists – then often warmly regarded in progressive circles – took the view that young working-class women should not be submitting themselves to urban dangers and indignities. Instead they should profit from growing prosperity and sanitary science, stay at home in the suburbs, and breed a healthier race than the scrawny weaklings whose enfeebled physique had shocked the nation at the time of recruitment for the Boer War.

4.48 Working in
the Clement's Inn
headquarters of the
Women's Social and
Political Union, 1911.
(LSE Library)

There is of course another side to the story. Among the factors behind the upsurge of suffragism in these years lay a sense of independence and solidarity fostered by the growth in women's employment, however poorly paid, and women's ability to escape home, no matter what the restrictions. The images of the London suffragettes – organising and printing propaganda in their offices (fig.4.48) as well as demonstrating in the streets – are a reminder that this famous symptom of contemporary turbulence could only follow from a confidence in working, living and public appearances unfamiliar to respectable Victorian women. If the leadership came from self-assured, well-off ladies from the upper middle class, their foot soldiers had learnt freedoms that their mothers lacked.

Militant suffragism was a slow starter in London. The Women's Social and Political Union was founded in 1903, but only after 1906 did it start to make much impact on the capital. The bulk of dramatic events – the arson attacks (sports pavilions were the commonest target), the imprisonments and force feedings, the Cat and Mouse Act, the 'martyrdom' of Emily Davidson and so on – took place in 1912–13.

Women's greater ease and freedom also helped fuel the Edwardian shopping boom. Women had always done most of the shopping; women's draperies dominated London's major shopping streets and underlay the origins of the department stores. Now they had quicker and safer means of transport to these establishments, whose aggrandisement was underwritten by their purchases. Special trains brought shoppers in to visit the trio of big stores in Kensington High Street: Barkers, Derry and Toms, and Pontings. The growth of Harrods in Brompton Road, Whiteleys in Queensway, and Arding and Hobbs at Clapham Junction was likewise dependent on proximity to stations. Arnold Bennett took the inflation of these emporia as the subject of *Hugo* (1906), one of the 'fantasias' that he interpolated between his serious novels. From the height of a glass dome over the bloated store he has created in Sloane Street, Hugo the eponymous hero looks down on the ladies and shop assistants scurrying about below and congratulates himself on his opulence and organisation.

In this heyday of the department store, Oxford Street came to the fore. The opening in 1900 of the Central Line boosted the street's vitality and prosperity, with four stops at close intervals along its length. Oxford Street had been fashionable since the eighteenth century, when it mainly serviced the residents of Mayfair and Marylebone. The sense of a centre on which shoppers converged from afar had been confirmed well before the Tube arrived. For some time, Oxford

4.49 Bourne and Hollingsworth, Oxford Street, in 1902. The shop occupied the lower floors only of a new-built block. The upper floors were probably flats. (Christopher Bourne)

Street's leading shops had been expanding fast, usually converting themselves into limited companies in order to raise more capital. Those that now rebuilt with a fresh scale and coherence included John Lewis, D.H. Evans, Peter Robinson, Waring and Gillow, and Bourne and Hollingsworth. Last in the sequence came Selfridges (1908–9), exceptional because it started from scratch.

The growth of two of these department stores, forgotten today, is worth following. First, Bourne and Hollingsworth. Walter Bourne and Howard Hollingsworth were cousins who had learnt the drapery trade in Birmingham before setting up together in Westbourne Grove. In 1901 they transferred into two units of a newly completed speculative block in Oxford Street (fig.4.49). They

4.50 Waring and Gillow building, Oxford Street, front in 2019. R. Frank Atkinson, architect, 1904–6. (Chris Redgrave for Historic England, DP 251202)

then took over shop after neighbouring shop, until by 1914 they occupied the whole block frontage. But at first the upper floors were mostly occupied by flats, as was still then common in London. When Harrods rebuilt between 1901 and 1912, flats were planned at first above first-floor level but then speedily absorbed into the store. For similar reasons Bourne and Hollingsworth rebuilt its whole site in the 1920s. Following trends long prevalent in France and America, shopping space in London was leaping belatedly upwards. Lifts for shoppers were now commonplace; escalators (Harrods had a primitive moving belt from 1898) were to follow.

Waring and Gillow, opened in 1906, occupied all of its eight storeys from the start. Untypically, it was a furniture and decorative emporium, not a clothes shop. Samuel Waring was an insatiable entrepreneur. His business stretched to big contracts for fitting out hotels, liners and theatres, and a half-share in the construction company which built the Ritz Hotel and a big chunk of Aldwych. His Oxford Street store was planned to house his retailing arm and advertise his empire. It was all erected in one go, as other department stores never were – even Selfridges was built in chunks. The site filled a full urban block, at a cool rent from the Howard de Walden Estate of £35,000 a year. The building (fig.4.50), in an overblown version of the 'Wrenaissance' style then just going out of date, ran to exhibition space, period rooms from Tudor to Late Georgian, reading rooms and other facilities. A dab hand at publicity, Waring solicited visits by foreign potentates, notably Kaiser Wilhelm II of Germany, who hired him to supply interiors for his yachts. When the Kaiser came in 1907, a banner was hung over the entrance reading 'Blood is thicker than water'.

Waring's *folie de grandeur* nearly broke him. He was to recover his fortunes by means of big war contracts for equipment used against his old patron, thanks to which he acquired one of Lloyd George's notorious peerages. That, if anything, is how he is remembered today, not as one of London's great shopping moguls. Yet his store foreshadowed Selfridges at the other end of Oxford Street in scale and ambition; probably Waring introduced Gordon Selfridge to London.

* * *

What of London's poor? Charles Masterman, quoted at the start of this chapter, was troubled by how they lived. Yet their lot was improving. The overall mortality rate in the County of London dropped from 20.9 per thousand in the early 1880s to 16.1 per thousand in the early 1900s, and then sharply to 12.7 per thousand in 1910, the lowest figure yet recorded, marking a decrease of one third over about thirty

4.51 'Family Life on a Pound a Week'. The original version of Maud Pember Reeves's *Round About a Pound a Week*, published as a Fabian tract in 1913. The ministering angel/social researcher knocks at the front door of the needy.

years. These figures were 'noticeably better than those for other large English cities, other European capitals and New York'. Infant mortality in particular was on the decline. Measures of income and deprivation, though always contested, point the same way. Perhaps the most absorbing survey of poverty ever published is Maud Pember Reeves's *Round About a Pound a Week*, issued as a Fabian Tract in 1913 after years of visits to households in Vauxhall and Kennington (fig.4.51). She chronicles hard lives and frequent crises but also much pride, independence and good cheer. Her account is far from the Victorian picture of 'immiseration' and despair.

At last the trojan efforts of the previous century were yielding fruit. The eradication of smallpox through compulsory vaccination marked one step forward; another was the enforcement of laws against adulterating food. Better housing and better education – the latter leading to wider understanding about health and diet – must have helped. Workhouses, still dire enough, had improved since Oliver Twist's day and were now partly hospitals.

Lower densities also helped. Slum districts of central London like St Giles and southern Clerkenwell became less benighted in proportion to the drop in their populations. The many missions in St Giles found less to do after 1900 and some were wound up. Three board schools had been built in the parish, superseding the primitive ragged schools of the 1840s and '50s. All were losing intake fast by 1900, as families drifted away; one was turned into an industrial school which taught printing. After the First World War, depopulation was to create severe difficulties for such districts. But for the time being the new borough authorities that had taken them over from the vestries could slacken the reins of relief a little and take breath.

The age-old argument about whether poverty was better alleviated by self-help or by root-and-branch intervention came to a head in the Royal Commission on the Poor Laws, which sat from 1905 and reported in 1909. This long-drawn-out enquiry became the stage for a showdown between two professional couples – all four ardent social reformers. Bernard and Helen Bosanquet championed the ideals of the conservative Charity Organisation Society, which boasted more than thirty years' experience in co-ordinating voluntary methods of poor relief; Beatrice and Sidney Webb fought for the abolition of the whole existing Poor Law system. In a sign of changing times the wives sat on the Commission, while their husbands contributed from the sidelines. In the short term the Webbs and their allies on the Commission lost. But their minority report, arguing for a structural understanding of poverty, was to become hallowed as an early step towards a welfare state. The cautious majority fared little better, as their report was largely set aside by the Liberal Government, which tackled some of the basic causes of poverty by means of two epoch-making measures – Asquith's Old Age Pensions Act of 1908 and Lloyd George's National Insurance Act of 1911.

* * *

London's public architecture was at high tide in the years after 1900. Its common idiom was Classicism, its common material the cool Portland stone that had been the capital's first choice for formal buildings since St Paul's Cathedral. Seldom remarked, the switch to Portland stone fronts along major London streets at this time in place of brick or terracotta seems to have started as a policy on Crown-owned property in the 1880s, for instance at the west end of Piccadilly. It gathered pace around 1900 and lasted right through the first half of the twentieth century, until the stark concrete and glass of the 1960s crushed it.

This architecture retained some of its English eccentricities but had ceased to be aloofly insular. Beaux-Arts styles and methods of design from France were welcomed in (more so after the Entente Cordiale of 1904 softened centuries of enmity), alongside elements from the 'City Beautiful' movement, one of the many Edwardian importations from America. It was all part of a worldwide consensus in urban architecture that lasted for the first quarter of the new century. In effect this was the earliest version of an 'international style' – a convergent counterpart to the divergent national idioms then popular everywhere for rural and suburban locations.

Above all, buildings looked good because money was lavished on them, in tacit agreement that architectural display was a mark of urban civilisation. Monumentality was perhaps to be expected from public buildings at the centres of power like the Old Bailey (fig.4.52), the War Office in Whitehall, the new Government Offices facing Parliament Square, and their neighbour, the Middlesex Guildhall. Understandably too, the rash of town halls built to dignify the creation of the London boroughs in 1900 rose to richer display than their predecessors. The finest, all in fruity Classical styles, can be found south of the river, at Deptford (fig.4.53), Lambeth and Woolwich – to which may be added the LCC's County Hall, challenging the Palace of Westminster's outdated Gothic across the Thames. More surprisingly, bank and insurance executives concurred and competed in this expenditure. Outdoing them all was the storeowner Gordon Selfridge who, to the chagrin of his Oxford Street rivals, created in Selfridges the world's noblest shopfront (fig.4.54). Was it a manifesto for civic values or a salesman's spectacular stunt for advertising his wares? In Edwardian terms the two are inseparable.

4.52 Central Criminal Court, Old Bailey, the *salle des pas perdus* under the dome.
E.W. Mountford, architect, 1902–7. Sculpture in the pendentives by F.W. Pomeroy.

4.53 Deptford Town Hall. Lanchester, Stewart and Rickards, architects, 1904–5. (Historic England Archive, BL19163)

It is usual to call this explosion of showy buildings the architecture of Imperial London. Imperial aspirations were doubtless involved. But it was also about a city bursting to express its pride after years of struggle with the vicious downside of its monstrous growth.

The West End and West Central areas saw a concentration of these efforts. In three locations an attempt was made to go beyond mere architecture and carry through a coherent urbanistic scheme of a kind only once before achieved in London, by John Nash's Regent Street. Easiest to implement, because little demolition was involved, was the recasting of The Mall, with the Victoria Memorial at one end and the Admiralty Arch at the other, a project that lasted from 1903 to 1911. This, the work of one architect, Aston Webb, followed a competition held after Queen Victoria's death. The scheme bears the impersonal competence typical of Webb's work, but the memorial itself, sculpted by Thomas Brock, has superlative French brio. Not all the surrounding gates and colonnades

4.54 Selfridges,
original section of
the Oxford Street
front. D.H. Burnham
and Co. with Francis
Swales and R. Frank
Atkinson, architects,
1907–9. (Historic England
Archive, BL20507)

could be completed, as the Dominion countries pressed to subscribe for them proved reluctant. The one weak point is Webb's insipid refronting of Buckingham Palace, carried out as a hasty afterthought (fig.4.55).

Trickier were the Crown Estate's plans for reshaping the central sections of Regent Street, where the original leases were running out and the shops looked shabby and outdated. These were to be replaced with bigger, more coherent stone-fronted buildings and shops on the old footprint except at Piccadilly Circus, which had been smashed up when Shaftesbury Avenue broke into one side a generation earlier and cried out for replanning. The Crown decided to employ the veteran Norman Shaw, but his designs for the noblest part of Regent Street, the curving Quadrant, proved costly and impractical. Shaw's strength was unequal to the ensuing battles with the shopkeepers, and only a fragment of his vision could be built in 1905–8. The scheme was rescued after the First World War by a committee of architects led by Reginald Blomfield, who pushed through an intelligent compromise design for the Quadrant. Further up Regent Street, some reconstruction started before the war, notably at Oxford Circus, begun in 1911 to a design in the Louis XVI taste. Piccadilly Circus, its counterpart in Nash's original plans, has never been redeemed.

The great trial of strength for Edwardian civic planning was the LCC's Kingsway-Aldwych development. This started out as an old-style project inherited from years back, devised to combine slum clearance with improvements to London's poor north-south communications. The LCC's decision to add in a tram tunnel and line the frontages with monumental architecture transformed it into a venture in modern urbanism. The 'Holborn to Strand' scheme was finally pushed through Parliament in 1899, thanks to the political skills of George Shaw Lefevre, a veteran of London planning battles. Buying and clearing sites (fig.4.56) caused the usual delays, followed by a botched attempt to impose uniform fronts round the sweep of Aldwych, the boldest gesture in the plan. The LCC then put off potential tenants by charging steep ground rents in an effort to recoup the costs of the clearances. As is the way with tightly controlled schemes of architecture, sites lay vacant for years; the whole was finished only in the 1930s.

Even so, the overall result was impressive and has never had the respect it deserves. It can boast five masterpieces of architecture, all in different variants of Classicism. At the west end was the Morning Post Building for the

4.55 The Victoria Memorial and the new front of Buckingham Palace, c.1914, before the installation of the bronze groups round the memorial. (Historic England Archive, SAM01/01/0058)

4.56 (left) Kingsway under construction in 1905. The picture shows the width of demolition and the steel decking for the roadway over the tram tunnel. The tunnel in the foreground is probably for services. (Collage 134730)

4.57 (below) Aldwych from the west in 1908, with the Morning Post Building left foreground, the Waldorf Hotel in the centre and the Gaiety Theatre to right. (Historic England Archive, BL20208)

conservative newspaper of that name (fig.4.57); at the answering east end, the General Accident Assurance Building (fig.4.58); and facing the latter, Australia House. On the west side of Kingsway was the British headquarters of the Kodak Company, in a cut-down version of the American skyscraper idiom; while further north, looking like an exile from Rome, came the concave-fronted Holy Trinity, Kingsway, London's only fully Classical Anglican church of the day (fig.4.59).

Remarkably, Scottish architects designed four of these five buildings. With good building stones close to hand, Scotland's Victorian cities had long boasted superior monumental architecture to London's, while Scots had embraced Beaux-Arts disciplines before the lackadaisical English. John Burnet of Glasgow, supreme in this field, had been invited down to design the northern extension of the British Museum. The General Accident building was his; the Kodak Building was carried out under his name by his brilliant young assistant, Thomas Tait; and Holy Trinity was mostly the work of J.J. Joass, who had also studied in Burnet's office. The exception was the Morning Post Building,

4.58 General Buildings, Aldwych, in October 1914. The General Accident Assurance Corporation's offices, built to designs by John Burnet in 1909–10, were used during the First World War to house the War Refugees' Committee and a Belgian labour office. (Historic England Archive, BL22817/009)

designed by Arthur Davis of Mewès and Davis in the polished French manner then popular internationally.

Only the fifth of these compositions is palpably imperial. That is Australia House, by the Aberdonian architects A. Marshall Mackenzie and Son. It is also the most assertive of the bunch, commanding the eastern corner of Aldwych in an outburst of pomp and symbolic sculpture (fig.4.60). Australia is not a country associated with monumentality, but it had its reasons for pulling out the stops here, as Eileen Chanin has explained in an absorbing study.

Surprisingly, this was London's first purpose-built embassy. Houses in fashionable quarters had usually sufficed for foreign diplomats. But the nations born out of Britain's old white settler colonies were in a rather different position. Once they attained formal recognition as independent dominions, they needed strategic representation in London to carry on the bargaining with the mother country that still perforce took place over trade, defence and migration. While Canada had been confederated back in 1867, the disparate colonies of Australia were pulled together only in 1901. Both had previously made do with poky premises in Victoria Street. Aldwych, sited astride the Strand – the line of communication between the City and Whitehall – was far better located. The rival Canadians thought about moving there but ducked out. Then after the State of Victoria opened a bureau on a corner of the future Australia House site in 1909, the new federal government joined in on the act. The extravagant project, completed only in 1918, represented partly an act of assertion in the face of bickering between the states back home, partly the urge to outface Canada in London. To a degree the gesture worked. Other dominions and colonies went on to locate their high commissions along the same route: the Indians also in Aldwych, the Canadians and South Africans in Trafalgar Square. Later, the Rhodesians took a fine building just off the Strand originally designed for the British Medical Association by Charles Holden; it is now Zimbabwe House.

Since Edwardian London boasted so many outstanding public buildings, a few words about other designs by the leading architects at Kingsway-Aldwych must stand for the rest. Arthur Davis's Ritz Hotel of 1903–6 became London's landmark of Edwardian cosmopolitanism. Two brilliantly nervous designs by Joass, the Royal Insurance Building in Piccadilly and Mappin and Webb's shop in Oxford Street, both completed in 1908, are good metaphors for Edwardian restlessness; they take their cue from Michelangelo, jumpiest of great architects. By contrast, Burnet preferred strength and confidence. His noble north front to the British Museum has been mentioned; even finer is the great staircase within.

4.59 Holy Trinity, Kingsway. Belcher and Joass, architects, 1910–11. (Chris Redgrave)

4.60 Australia House
with Victory Parade,
3 May 1919. St Mary le
Strand to left, Aldwych
to right. A. Marshall
Mackenzie and Son,
architects. (Eileen
Chanin)

Not everyone welcomed this onslaught of the new. As always, second-rate
architecture outstripped the best in quantity. With all the money lavished on
development came much crudity and destruction. Old and lovely buildings
succumbed, particularly in the City. Though the preservation movement was
stirring following William Morris's emotive lead, its practical influence in
rampant London was weak. There were still no laws to safeguard places of beauty
and historic interest. Threatened with destruction, the fifteenth-century Crosby
Hall was transferred from the City after great efforts and rebuilt in 1909–10 as
part of a hall of residence for London University on the Chelsea Embankment
(fig.4.61). The Kingsway-Aldwych scheme likewise destroyed much that was
picturesque and venerable but shabby. Laurence Gomme, the LCC's Clerk to the
Council and a believer in the practical lessons of history, at least managed to get
parts of it recorded by means of the Survey of London series, which the LCC had
rescued after Ashbee, its founder, lost interest.

Among the protesters against everyday destruction and redevelopment was
E.M. Forster. His *Howards End*, published in 1910, is freighted with regrets for the loss
of old places and old ways, and dire warnings against cosmopolitanism, personified
by the heartless African rubber mogul Mr Wilcox. At a poignant moment in the
book, the Schlegel sisters are obliged to leave their cherished Marylebone home
because their landlord plans to build 'Babylonian flats' on the site. Mrs Wilcox, the
mysterious psychological force at the centre of the novel, protests:

It is monstrous, Miss Schlegel; it isn't right. I had no idea that this was hanging over you. I do pity you from the bottom of my heart. To be parted from your house, your father's house – it oughtn't to be allowed. It is worse than dying. I would rather die than – Oh, poor girls! Can what they call civilisation be right if people mayn't die in the room where they were born?

But Mrs Wilcox does die just a few pages later – and not in the house where she was born.

*   *   *

4.61 Crosby Hall as rebuilt in Chelsea, 1909–10, as part of 'More's Garden', intended as a hall of residence for the new Imperial College. (Collage 55947)

Edward VII's coronation in 1902, the first for 64 years, had to be postponed for two months following the King's illness. No matter. The new reign, when it got going, was marked by a level of consumption and ceremonial unheard of in the

4.62 Decorations in Whitehall for the Coronation of George V, June 1911. On the extreme left a stand is being erected. (Historic England Archive, MCF01/02/0219)

days of the old Queen. Encouraged by the hedonistic monarch, these were the halcyon years of the London Season, an upper-class social extravaganza covering about half of every year. Its elaborate observances and accompanying sideshows enriched and animated the capital.

No let-up was anticipated when George V came to the throne. For his coronation in 1911 officials could learn from the earlier event. This time the public manifestation of the monarch and his consort went beyond the short procession from the Palace to the Abbey and back via the usual ceremonial streets. Separate parades elsewhere in London took place on subsequent days, while co-ordinated schemes of plaster decorations, bunting and illuminations for the main streets were commissioned from artists for the first time. The painter Frank Brangwyn, for instance, designed a scheme for New Bond Street and a special ceremonial arch in Whitehall on the government of New Zealand's behalf (fig.4.62). Under the headline 'A Transformed City', *The Times* waxed pompous in face of the imperial pageantry on Coronation Day:

> Nothing mean or unlovely was to be seen in the grey capital of the Empire. With a touch of her wand the fairy godmother electricity had turned her into a ravishing princess. She was crowned with light, as her King had been crowned earlier in the day.

But the bright promise of the new reign was belied. A time of turbulence followed, often erupting on London's streets: struggles with the suffragettes, strikes, murderous confrontations with Latvian anarchists at Houndsditch and Sidney Street, a long and bitter constitutional crisis over the power of the Lords, and the looming partition of Ireland. Two Post-Impressionist exhibitions rustled the cultural dovecotes. Looking back, Virginia Woolf pronounced that 'on or about December 1910 human character changed'.

To cap all this came the international crisis, gathering tornado-like in the summer of 1914. Just before the storm broke, there came a moment of stillness and hush in central London. Charles Masterman (fig.4.63) caught it:

I remember a few days later coming out from conferences in which, within, we realised that the end had come, to find under the hot August sunlight, great crowds of silent men and women crowding Whitehall, and all the way from Downing Street to Parliament, just waiting, hour after hour, in a kind of awe and expectation, to know whether the world in which they had lived and moved all their lives had ceased to exist.

It had. London would never be the centre of the world again.

4.63 Charles Masterman arriving at Parliament on the eve of the First World War.

Sources and References

This list is confined to the main books and articles I have used and to sources of quotations. Much more can be found now on many excellent websites.

CHAPTER 1

Grant and Kensington House. *Survey of London*, vol. 42, 1986; *Dictionary of Business Biography*.

Anthony Trollope, *The Way We Live Now*, 1874–5, quotations from Chapters 31 and 74.

Doré and Thomson. Gustave Doré and Blanchard Jerrold, *London: A Pilgrimage*, 1872; J. Thomson and Adolphe Smith, *Street Life in London*, 1877, originally published in monthly parts, reprinted as *Victorian Street Life in Historic Photographs*, 1994.

Munby. Derek Hudson, *Munby, Man of Two Worlds: The Life and Diaries of Arthur J. Munby*, 1972, quotation from diary entry, 31 December 1870.

Grosvenor Gallery, etc. Colleen Denney, *At the Temple of Art: The Grosvenor Gallery, 1877–1890*, 2000; Elizabeth Prettejohn, *Art for Art's Sake*, 2007.

The Garretts. Agnes and Rhoda Garrett, *Suggestions for House Decoration in Painting, Woodwork and Furniture*, 1876; Jo Manton, *Elizabeth Garrett Anderson*, 1965.

Skating. Newspapers, 1875–6; Wikipedia for John Gamgee and the Glaciarium; *Survey of London*, vol. 53, 2020, for Oxford Street rink.

Metropolitan Board of Works. Sir Gwilym Gibbon and Reginald W. Bell, *History of the London County Council 1889–1939*, 1939; Francis Sheppard, *London, 1808–1870: The Infernal Wen*, 1971; David Owen, *The Government of Victorian London, 1855–1889*, 1982.

Urban improvements. Percy J. Edwards, *History of London Street Improvements, 1855–1897*, 1898; Owen, op. cit.

Housing. John Nelson Tarn, *Five Per Cent Philanthropy*, 1973; Anthony S. Wohl, *The Eternal Slum*, 1977.

Metropolitan Asylums Board. Gwendoline M. Ayers, *England's First State Hospitals and the Metropolitan Asylums Board, 1867–1930*, 1971.

School Board for London. Stuart Maclure, *One Hundred Years of London Education, 1870–1970*, 1970; Mark Girouard, *Sweetness and Light*, 1977; Deborah E.B. Weiner, *Architecture and Social Reform in Late-Victorian London*, 1994; Robin Betts, *Powerful and Splendid: The London School Board 1870–1904*, 2015.

'No equally powerful body': *The Times*, 29 November 1870.

'Each school stands up': Charles Booth, *Life and Labour of the People in London*, 1st series, East London, vol. 1, 1889–91, p. 129.

Battersea. *Survey of London*, vols 49 and 50, quotations about Shaftesbury Park, vol. 50, p. 271.

'One of the hottest metropolitan potatoes': F.M.L. Thompson, *Hampstead: Building a Borough 1650–1964*, 1974, p. 135.

Estates. Grosvenor Estate, *Survey of London*, vol. 39; Portland Estate, *Survey of London*, vol. 51, introduction.

Edward Yates. H.J. Dyos, *Victorian Suburb*, 1961, pp. 127–37.

Alfred Heaver. Wikipedia article; *Survey of London*, vol. 50.

Archibald Cameron Corbett. *Archibald Cameron Corbett: The Man and the Houses* (film), 2018.

'The Estate became': Simon Jenkins, *Landlords to London: The Story of a Capital and its Growth*, 1975, p. 120.

'The power possessed': Frank Banfield, *The Great Landlords of London*, [1888], p. 34.

Onslow Gardens. *Survey of London*, vol. 41.

De Vere Gardens. *Survey of London*, vol. 42, 'always in excess of the residents' needs': p. 128.

'Horses are hard work': F.M.L. Thompson, *Victorian England: The Horse-Drawn Society*, 1970.

Redcliffe Square and Cornwall Gardens. *Survey of London*, vols 41 and 42.

Queen Anne in Belsize Park. John Summerson, 'The London Suburban Villa 1850–1880' in *The Unromantic Castle*, 1990.

Artists' houses. Giles Walkley, *Artists' Houses in London 1764–1914*, 1994.

Ernest George. Hilary J. Grainger, *The Architecture of Sir Ernest George*, 2011.

Norman Shaw. Andrew Saint, *Richard Norman Shaw*, 2nd ed., 2010.

Bedford Park. Margaret Jones Bolsterli, *The Early Community at Bedford Park*, 1977; T. Affleck Greeves and Peter Murray, *Bedford Park: The First Garden Suburb*, 3rd ed., 2010; D.W. Budworth, *Jonathan Carr's Bedford Park*, 2012; Andrew Saint, *Bedford Park, Radical Suburb*, 2016.

CHAPTER 2

Marx's death and memorial. Yvonne Kapp, *Eleanor Marx*, vol. 1, 1972; Maximilian Rubel and Margaret Manale, *Marx without Myth*, 1975; Highgate Cemetery Newsletter, April 2018.

Hyndman. Henry Mayers Hyndman, *The Record of an Adventurous Life*, 1911, 'a powerful, shaggy, untamed old man': p. 269; 'The Dawn of a Revolutionary Epoch': p. 226; selling *Justice* on street corners, p. 333.

Early socialism in London. Paul Thompson, *Socialists, Liberals and Labour*, 1967; E.P. Thompson, *William Morris: Romantic to Revolutionary*, rev. ed., 1977.

Henry George. Charles Albro Barker, *Henry George*, 1955, 'He spoke of Liberty': pp. 375–6; Elwood P. Lawrence, *Henry George in the British Isles*, 1957, 'a bump of reverence': p. 6.

John Burns. Joseph Burgess, *John Burns: The Rise and Progress of a Right Honourable*, 1911; William Kent, *John Burns, Labour's Lost Leader*, 1950; Kenneth D. Brown, *John Burns*, 1977.

Trafalgar Square demonstrations. Gareth Stedman Jones, *Outcast London*, 1971; Rodney Mace, *Trafalgar Square*, 1976, 'huddled together on the seats': p. 171; Sean Creighton in Keith Flett (ed.), *A History of Riots*, 2015; newspapers.

Burns speeches. 'A waste of good rope . . . Unless we get bread', *The Standard*, 7 April 1886.

Poverty, slums and unemployment. The classic 'miserabilist' text is Gareth Stedman Jones, *Outcast London*, 1971, Chapter 3 for Mayhew's calculation.

Mearns, Sims and *How the Poor Live*. George R. Sims, *My Life: Sixty Years' Recollections of Bohemian London*, 1917. Mearns's authorship of *The Bitter Cry of Outcast London* was disputed by W.C. Preston.

W.T. Stead. Estelle W. Stead, *My Father: Personal and Spiritual Reminiscences*, 1913; Frederick Whyte, *The Life of W.T. Stead*, 2 vols, 1925.

Jack the Ripper reaction. L. Perry Curtis Jr, *Jack the Ripper and the London Press*, 2001; 'Nightly fears and fantasies': Compton Mackenzie, *My Life and Times, Octave One: 1883–1891*, 1963, pp. 164–5.

'Two millions': Walter Besant, *All Sorts and Conditions of Men*, 1882, Chapter 1. The other novels of note were Mrs Humphry Ward, *Robert Elsmere*, 1888; John Law (Margaret Harkness), *Out of Work*, 1888, and *In Darkest London*, 1889; Israel Zangwill, *Children of the Ghetto*, 1892; Arthur Morrison, *A Child of the Jago*, 1896; and Jack London, *The People of the Abyss*, 1903.

'They came oftener': Henry James, *The Princess Casamassima*, 1886, Chapter 21.

St Cuthbert's, Philbeach Gardens. *Survey of London*, vol. 42.

Holy Redeemer, Clerkenwell. *Survey of London*, vol. 47.

'In 1880 the air of England': C.R.L. Fletcher, *Edmond Warre*, 1922, p. 137.

St Giles-in-the-Fields. Research by Rebecca Preston and the author for a social history of the parish, 2019–21.

'A passionate desire to reform the world', etc.: William Hale White, *Mark Rutherford's Deliverance*, 1885, Chapter 2.

David Rice-Jones. Rev. D. Rice-Jones, *In the Slums*, 1884; author's researches.

Mrs Humphry Ward and *Robert Elsmere*. John Sutherland, *Mrs Humphry Ward, Eminent Victorian, Pre-eminent Edwardian*, 1991.

The settlement movement. Asa Briggs and Anne Macartney, *Toynbee Hall*, 1984; W.J. Fishman, *East End 1888*, 1988; José Harris, *William Beveridge*, rev. ed., 1997; Nigel Scotland, *Squires in the Slums*, 2007; Survey of London, draft by Aileen Reid for Whitechapel volumes, 2020.

'The principle of our work': quoted in Fishman, op. cit., p. 230.

'It seems to us': quoted in Fishman, op. cit., p. 301.

'Amid the laundries': Scotland, op. cit., p. 111.

Salvation Army. Glen K. Horridge, *The Salvation Army: Origins and Early Days*, 1993.

Charles Booth. T.S. and M.B. Simey, *Charles Booth: Social Scientist*, 1960, 'at all times more or less in want': p. 90; 'Founder of the science of cities': on a foundation stone, former Browning Settlement, Walworth Road.

Criticism of Booth's findings. Michael Ball and David Sunderland, *An Economic History of London 1800–1914*, 2001, pp. 111–13.

Sweating. Stedman Jones, op. cit., Chapter 5; Fishman, op. cit., Chapter 3; Ball and Sunderland, op. cit., pp. 294–5.

East End immigration and Jews. Fishman, op. cit.; Cecil Bloom, 'The Politics of Immigration 1881–1905' in *Jewish Historical Studies*, vol. 33, 1992–4; 'Arnold White and Sir William Evans-Gordon: Their Involvement in Immigration in Late-Victorian and Edwardian Britain', ibid., vol. 39, 2004.

'Into the heart of East London': Zangwill, op. cit., proem.

'As a citizen': Beatrice Webb, *My Apprenticeship*, 1979 ed., pp. 443–4.

'The one practical outcome': quoted in Simey, op. cit., p. 109.

'Millions of tons': George Gissing, *The Nether World*, 1889, Chapter 30.

Cheap Trains. H.J. Dyos, 'Workmen's Fares in South London, 1860–1914' in *Journal of Transport History*, 1953, reprinted in *Exploring the Urban Past*, ed. David Cannadine and David Reeder, 1992; T.C. Barker and Michael Robbins, *A History of London Transport*, vol. 1, 1963, Chapter 7; Robert Thorne, *Liverpool Street Station*, 1978; Ball and Sunderland, op. cit., pp. 248–50.

Octavia Hill. Gillian Darley, *Octavia Hill*, 1990.

City charities and the City Parochial Foundation. Victor Belcher, *The City Parochial Foundation 1891–1991*, 1991, 'of whom but four or five': p. 20; 'Breakfast and dinner': p. 9.

Regent Street Polytechnic. Ethel M. Hogg, *Quintin Hogg*, 1907; Helen Glew et al., *Educating the Mind, Body and Spirit: The Legacy of Quintin Hogg and the Polytechnic, 1864–1992*, 2013; *Survey of London*, vol. 52.

The LCC and the polytechnics. Andrew Saint, 'Technical Education and the Early LCC' in *Politics and the People of London*, 1989; *Survey of London*, vol. 49, for Battersea Polytechnic.

People's Palace. Deborah E.B. Weiner, *Architecture and Social Reform in Late-Victorian London*, 1994, Chapter 7.

Telephones. F.G.C. Baldwin, *The History of the Telephone in the United Kingdom*, 1925; Ball and Sunderland, op. cit., pp. 284–6.

Electric lighting. Robert Hammond, *The Electric Light in our Homes*, 1884; Graeme Gooday, *Domesticating Electricity*, 2008; Gavin Weightman, *Children of Light*, 2011; Ball and Sunderland, op. cit., pp. 277–81.

Exhibitions. *Survey of London*, vol. 38, 'Already a failure': p. 224.

Earl's Court Exhibition. *Survey of London*, vol. 42, 1986, 'The Indian babies': p. 332.

'Covering in the 48 hours': *Illustrated Police News*, 19 November 1887.

CHAPTER 3

Dowson. Jad Adams, *Madder Music, Stronger Wine: The Life of Ernest Dowson, Poet and Decadent*, 2000; *The Letters of Ernest Dowson*, ed. Desmond Flower and Henry Maas, 1967. 'We dined': Adams, p. 101; 'though I hate London': *Letters*, p. 270.

'Much of the fascination': Compton Mackenzie, *My Life and Times, Octave Two: 1891–1900*, 1963, p. 257.

Art cliques of the 1890s. William Rothenstein, *Men and Memories: Recollections, 1872–1900*, vol. 1, 1931.

Mackmurdo and the Century Guild. Stuart Evans, *Century Guild of Artists*, Oxford Art Online, 2008; and his thesis, 'Arthur Heygate Mackmurdo (1851–1942) and the Century Guild of Artists', University of Manchester, 1986; W.B. Yeats, *Memoirs*, 1972.

Wilde. Richard Ellmann, *Oscar Wilde*, 1987, 'aestheticism was revised': p. 288; 'one must shake off London life': p. 137.

'It is the problem of slavery': Oscar Wilde, *The Picture of Dorian Gray*, 1890, Chapter 3.

Rosebery's difficulties. David Brooks, *The Destruction of Lord Rosebery: From the Diary of Sir Edward Hamilton, 1894–1895*, 1987.

Beardsley. Matthew Sturgis, *Aubrey Beardsley, A Biography*, 1999; Stephen Calloway and Caroline Corbeau-Parsons, *Aubrey Beardsley*, 2020.

Kipling. Harry Ricketts, *The Unforgiving Minute: A Life of Rudyard Kipling*, 1999; Andrew Lycett, *Rudyard Kipling*, 1999; 'An evil-evil day': *The Letters of Rudyard Kipling*, vol. 1, 1872–89, ed. Thomas Pinney, 1990.

'There was no premonition': Mackenzie, *Octave Two*, op. cit., p. 175.

The Empire, Leicester Square. *Survey of London*, vol. 34, 1966; Peter Bailey, *Popular Culture and Performance in the Victorian City*, 1998; Joseph Donohue, *Fantasies of Empire: The Empire Theatre of Varieties and the Licensing Controversy of 1894*, 2005.

'Mrs Ormiston Chant faints': Mackenzie, *Octave Two*, op. cit., p. 135.

'Leisure activities could make': Michael Ball and David Sunderland, *An Economic History of London 1800–1914*, 2001, p. 168.

Pubs. Mark Girouard, *Victorian Pubs*, 1975, 'The pubs then': p. 10; 'The smash came': p. 182; 'From 1900': p. 186.

'In the days of my youth': Edmund Yates, *Fifty Years of London Life*, 1885, p. 99.

Restaurants and tea shops. George R. Sims, *My Life: Sixty Years' Recollections of Bohemian London*, 1917, p. 97; Brenda Assael, *The London Restaurant, 1840–1914*, 2018.

Lyons. Peter Bird, *The First Food Empire: A History of J. Lyons & Co.*, 2000.

Halls for classical music. Michael Forsyth, *Buildings for Music*, 1985.

The Queen's Hall. Robert Elkin, *Queen's Hall, 1893–1941*, 1944; *Survey of London*, vol. 52.

Wigmore Street recital halls. *Survey of London*, vol. 51.

'The atmosphere is laden with smoke': W.H. Hudson, *Birds in London*, 1898, Chapter 12.

Parks and the LCC. William Saunders, *History of the First London County Council, 1889 to 1891*, 1892, '25,000 persons': p. 223.

Sport and the Polytechnic. Mark Clapson, *An Education in Sport*, 2012.

'With a ten-mile spin': W.S. Gilbert, *Utopia Limited*, 1893, Act 2.

Football. Tony Mason, *Association Football and English Society, 1863–1915*, 1980; websites.

Thames Ironworks. Kirk Blows and Tony Hogg, *The Essential History of West Ham United*, 2000.

'Was becoming less insular': Sims, op. cit., pp. 95–7.

The press and the Harmsworth revolution. Richard Bourne, *Lords of Fleet Street: The Harmsworth Dynasty*, 1990; Susie Barson and Andrew Saint, *A Farewell to Fleet Street*, 1988, 'Every time': p. 14; 'makes it easier': p. 30.

The police. W.J. Fishman, *East End 1888*, 1988, Chapter 7, 'London is the safest capital': p. 178.

The early London County Council. Saunders, op. cit.; Sir Harry Haward, *The London County Council from Within*, 1932; Sir Gwilym Gibbon and Reginald W. Bell, *History of the London County Council 1889–1939*, 1939.

Libraries in London. Report by Roger Bowdler and Steven Brindle for English Heritage.

Later years of the School Board. Eric Eaglesham, *From School Board to Local Authority*,1956; Robin Betts, *Dr Macnamara, 1861–1931*, 1999; and his *Powerful and Splendid: The London School Board 1870–1904*, 2015.

The Technical Education Board. Saint, 'Technical Education and the Early LCC' in *Politics and the People of London*, 1989; 'A school of University rank': C.T. Millis, *Technical Education*, 1925, p. 87.

Frustrations of the early LCC. Saunders, op. cit.; Haward, op. cit.

Boundary Street and Millbank. R. Vladimir Steffel, 'The Boundary Street Estate', *Town Planning Review*, vol. 47, no. 2, 1976; Anthony S. Wohl, *The Eternal Slum*, 1977, Chapter 10; Susan Beattie, *A Revolution in London Housing*, 1980.

'Salisbury and Chamberlain aimed': John Davis, *Reforming London*, 1988, p. 202.

Town halls of the 1890s. Battersea, *Survey of London*, vol. 49; Clerkenwell, *Survey of London*, vol. 47, 'the smallest and worst': p. 125.

Arts and Crafts in London. Alastair Service, *Edwardian Architecture*, 1977; Alan Crawford, *C.R. Ashbee*, 1985; Peter Davey, *Arts and Crafts Architecture*, rev. ed., 1995.

Arts and Crafts in Mayfair. *Survey of London*, vols 39 and 40.

Westminster Cathedral. Peter Howell, *John Francis Bentley*, 2020, Chapter 12.

West Ham. John Marriott, 'West Ham: London's Industrial Centre and Gateway to the World I: Industrialization 1840–1910' in *London Journal*, vol. 13, no. 2, 1987; Jim Clifford, *West Ham and the River Lea*, 2017.

CHAPTER 4

'There is so much of us': C.F.G. Masterman, *From the Abyss*, 1902, p. 9; 'We live "in the buildings"': p. 33.

'For myself, when on a train': Ford Madox Hueffer, *The Soul of London*, 1905, p. 60.

'There are, say moralists': John Galsworthy, *Fraternity*, 1909, p. 298.

Railways and suburbanisation. John R. Kellett, *The Impact of Railways on Victorian Cities*, 1969; T.C. Barker and Michael Robbins, *A History of London Transport*, vol. 1, 1963, Chapter 7.

Doubling railway tracks and electrification: Barker and Robbins, op. cit., vol. 2, 1974, Chapter 7.

Street lighting to electric traction. Gavin Weightman, *Children of Light*, 2011.

The early tube railways: Barker and Robbins, op. cit., vol. 2, Chapter 3; B.G. Wilson and V. Stewart Haram, *The Central London Railway*, 1950; Michael Ball and David Sunderland, *An Economic History of London 1800–1914*, 2001, pp. 255–63.

Electric trams. Barker and Robbins, op. cit., vol. 2, Chapter 2; Ball and Sunderland, op. cit., pp. 249–55, 'a juggernaut': p. 255.

'Hesitant beginnings' and motorisation: Barker and Robbins, op. cit., vol. 2, Chapter 6.

London traffic. Royal Commission on London Traffic, vol. 7, 1905.

Car showrooms. Kathryn A. Morrison and John Minnis, *Carscapes*, 2012, Chapter 2.

Thames crossings. Bridget Cherry and Nikolaus Pevsner, *London 2: South*, 1983, pp. 707–16, provides a list with dates, contributed by Malcolm Tucker; Kenneth Powell, *Tower Bridge*, 2019.

Co-ordination of technical education. Andrew Saint, 'Technical Education and the LCC' in *Politics and the People of London*, 1989, Chapter 4.

LCC fire stations. John B. Nadal, *London's Fire Stations*, 2006.

Ilford and Golders Green. Alan A. Jackson, *Semi-Detached London*, 1973, Chapter 4.

Archibald Cameron Corbett. *Archibald Cameron Corbett: The Man and the Houses* (film), 2018.

Golders Green Crematorium. Percy C. Jupp and Hilary J. Grainger, *Golders Green Crematorium, 1902–2002*, 2002.

Hampstead Garden Suburb. Mervyn Miller and A. Stuart Gray, *Hampstead Garden Suburb*, 1992; Mervyn Miller, *Raymond Unwin: Garden Cities and Town Planning*, 1992; Raymond Unwin, *Town Planning in Practice*, 1909.

'In the afternoon': Lucy Masterman, *C.F.G. Masterman, a Biography*, 1939, p. 127.

LCC cottage estates. Susan Beattie, *A Revolution in London Housing*, 1980; Andrew Saint, 'Spread the People: The LCC's Dispersal Policy, 1889–1965' in *Politics and the People of London*, 1989, Chapter 12.

'Convenient, cheap and rapid transit': Chelsea Borough Council Minutes, 1902.

Water supply. John Broich, *London: Water and the Making of the Modern City*, 2013; Ball and Sunderland, op. cit., pp. 270–1.

'The Council has already lost': quoted in *Educational Record*, vol. 22, April 1929.

Industry in London. Ball and Sunderland, op. cit., pp. 57–66, 293–319; Peter Hall, *The Industries of London since 1861*, 1962; Geoff Marshall, *London's Industrial Heritage*, 2013.

Statistics of employees. Mostly from websites, but *Survey of London*, vol. 48, 2012, p. 176 gives figures for Woolwich Arsenal; J.D. Scott, *Siemens Brothers 1858–1958*, 1958, p. 193, for Siemens.

South Shoreditch. Joanna Smith and Ray Rogers, *Behind the Veneer: The South Shoreditch Furniture Trade and its Buildings*, 2006, quoting Peter Hall, 'Industrial London: A General View' in J.T. Coppock and H. Prince, *Greater London*, 1964.

Dispersal of industry. D.E. Keeble, *Industrial Decentralization and the Metropolis: The North-West London Case*, 1968.

Siemens' move to Stafford. Scott, op. cit., p. 75.

Industry in Clerkenwell. *Survey of London*, vol. 46, 2008, pp. 17–18; 'Played a crucial role': J.E. Martin, *Greater London: An Industrial Geography*, 1966, pp. 14, 35–6.

Port of London Authority. Sir Joseph G. Broodbank, *History of the Port of London*, 1921; David Kynaston, *The City of London: Vol. 2, The Golden Years*, 1995, pp. 343–5; Nigel Watson, *The Port of London Authority*, 2009.

'The telegraph abolished': Kynaston, op. cit., p. 261, quoting *The Statist*, 8 August 1903.

Clerks. Michael Heller, 'Work, Income and Stability: The Late Victorian and Edwardian London Male Clerk Revisited' in *Business History*, vol. 50, no. 3, 2008.

The City. Kynaston, op. cit., with statistics on pp. 242, 301 and 596, 'Crowds bubble': p. 240, quoting from P.F. William Ryan, 'Going to Business in London' in George R. Sims (ed.), *Living London*, vol. 1, 1901, p. 196.

'As the world's only free gold market': Kynaston, op. cit., p. 600.

'The professional peacemaker': Kynaston, op. cit., p. 385.

Proportion of women clerical workers. Ball and Sunderland, op. cit., p. 326.

Hostels for women. Emily Gee, '"Where shall she live?": Housing the New Working Woman in Late Victorian and Edwardian London' in Geoff Brandwood (ed.), *Living, Leisure and Law: Eight Building Types in England 1800–1941*, 2010.

Marylebone hostels. *Survey of London*, vol. 52, 2017.

Servant numbers. Ball and Sunderland, op. cit., p. 320.

Department stores. *Survey of London*, vols 41 (Harrods), 42 (Barkers, Derry and Toms, and Pontings), 49 (Arding and Hobbs), and 53 (the Oxford Street stores).

Samuel Waring. Andrew Saint, 'What Became of Waring? Fortunes of an Entrepreneur in Furnishing, Shopkeeping and Construction' in *Construction History*, vol. 29, no. 1, 2014, pp. 75–97.

Rates and causes of death. Mary Kilbourne Matossian, 'Death in London 1750–1909' in *Journal of Interdisciplinary Studies*, vol. 16, no. 2, 1985, pp. 183–97.

'Noticeably better': Ball and Sunderland, op. cit., p. 46.

Maud Pember Reeves, *Round About a Pound a Week*, new edition with introduction by Sally Alexander, 1979.

The Webbs, the Bosanquets and the Poor Law Commission. A.M. McBriar, *An Edwardian Mixed Doubles: The Bosanquets Versus the Webbs*, 1987.

Edwardian architecture. Alastair Service, *London 1900*, 1979.

The Victoria Memorial and the Mall. Report by Steven Brindle for English Heritage.

Rebuilding of Regent Street. Hermione Hobhouse, *Regent Street*, rev. ed., 2008; Andrew Saint, *Richard Norman Shaw*, 2nd ed., 2010, Chapter 9; *Survey of London*, vols 52 (Upper Regent Street) and 53 (Oxford Circus).

Kingsway-Aldwych. Charles Gordon, *Old Time Aldwych, Kingsway, and Neighbourhood*, 1903; James Winter, *London's Teeming Streets, 1830–1914*, 1993, conclusion, pp. 207–16.

Australia House. Eileen Chanin, *Capital Designs: Australia House and Visions of an Imperial London*, 2018.

Crosby Hall. Andrew Saint, 'Ashbee, Geddes, Lethaby and the Rebuilding of Crosby Hall' in *Architectural History*, vol. 34, 1991; *Survey of London*, vol. 3, 1911, on Lincoln's Inn Fields, recorded buildings affected by the Kingsway-Aldwych scheme.

'It is monstrous': E.M. Forster, *Howards End*, 1910, Chapter 10.

'Nothing mean': *The Times*, 23 June 1911.

'Human character changed': Virginia Woolf, *Mr Bennett and Mrs Brown*, 1924, p. 4.

'I remember a few days later': Lucy Masterman, op. cit.

Index

First published in 2021 by Lund Humphries

Lund Humphries
Office 3, Book House
261A City Road
London EC1V 1JX
UK
www.lundhumphries.com

978-1-84822-465-0

A Cataloguing-in-Publication record for this book is available from the British Library.

Cover jacket: Booth's *Descriptive Map of London Poverty*, 1898–9, showing parts of Lambeth
and Southwark, merged with an image of Siemens arc lights at Mansion House, 1881
(J.D. Scott, *Siemens Brothers 1858–1958*, 1958).

Copy edited by John Jervis
Page design by Crow Books
Set in Albertina MT and Fogtwo No.5
Printed in China